THE BLACK ISLE RAILWAY

THE MUIR OF ORD TO FORTROSE BRANCH

JACK KERNAHAN

Highland Railway Society

The station nameboard at Fortrose in LMS colours.
(H C Casserley)

Local people with long memories may recall the sound made by the locomotive struggling to take lengthy potato specials up the 1 in 60 climb out of Fortrose. These usually ran in the evening and left the goods yard empty. An animal pen can be seen in the foreground.

(John Mackenzie)

(Front Cover) Ex-Highland Railway 4-4-0 no 14399 (formerly HR no 3) Ben Wyvis being turned at Fortrose on 14th August 1948. Engines were always turned at Fortrose and Muir of Ord, although by the time this photograph was taken, the turntable at Fortrose took a lot of manual effort to move it. This procedure often attracted an audience of local school children.   *(James L Stevenson)*

© Jack Kernahan 2013
ISBN: 978 0 9545485 9 9

Published by the Highland Railway Society : www.hrsoc.org.uk.

Printed by Berforts Information Press, Eynsham, Oxfordshire, OX29 4JB

CONTENTS

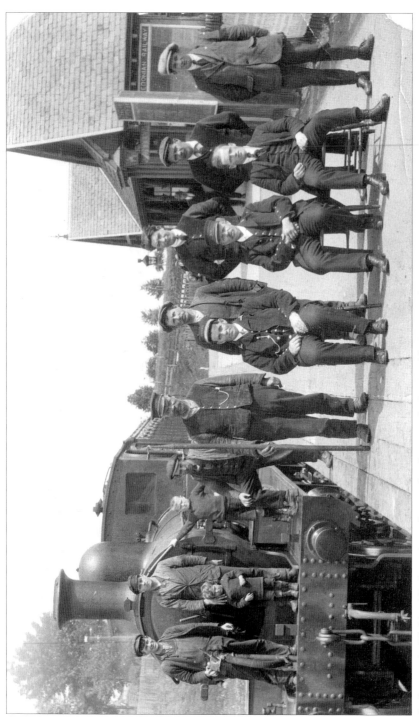

On loan to the Highland Railway due to locomotive shortages during World War 1, London & South Western Railway Adams Radial 4-4-2 tank no 0487 was photographed in 1919 at Fortrose with the station staff, including Kenneth Macdonald, station master, Jimmy Dick, booking clerk (who became station master at Fortrose in the 1940s), Ian Budge, fireman, Frankie Hay, driver (who was still a driver on the branch when passenger services ceased in 1951) and Jock Mackay (with shunting pole), pointsman from 1904 but by now porter/guard. The boys are Douglas and Albert Hay. William Macdonald, with black arm band following the death of his grandfather, is on the right.   (Courtesy Bill Forbes)

INTRODUCTION

For just over the first half of the twentieth century a branch line ran through the southern portion of the Black Isle, an area often described as neither black nor an isle! The richness of the soil results in the land producing a wonderful variety of colours, particularly greens, at every season of the year. While early transport difficulties meant that it was served more by sea than by land, it is a peninsula, bounded by the Cromarty Firth to the north and the Beauly and Moray Firths to the south.

As a peninsula it was not going to be on a direct line of railway and it is unlikely that a line would have been built had it not been for the fight between the rival Great North of Scotland and Highland Railways for a line to Inverness. Early local attempts produced much enthusiasm but insufficient funds and it was not until 1889 that an attempt by the Great North of Scotland to enter Inverness by both an indirect line from Elgin and an even more indirect route through the Black Isle forced the Highland Railway to build the Black Isle Railway. Even then the line went only as far as Fortrose. Original plans to reach Rosemarkie and Chanonry Point and suggestions that a continuation to Cromarty would be considered came to nothing.

The line became the typical country branch line, taking up to an hour for mixed trains to cover its thirteen miles. Friendships were made on the railway, which was an essential part of the community before the roads were sufficient to carry goods and passengers.

Today large lorries struggle through the narrow streets of Munlochy, Avoch, Fortrose and Rosemarkie, never designed for vehicles of such a size, while Fortrose enjoys a bus service almost twice every hour taking passengers into the heart of Inverness in less than 30 minutes. The railway is still fondly remembered by the senior citizens of the Black Isle and is a source of interest and enquiry for those who never knew it. Much has disappeared, but parts are still lovingly maintained, such as the beautifully restored Redcastle station building and the path along the trackbed between Fortrose and Avoch, carefully cleared of leaves every autumn by Colin Miller.

This history tells of the attempts to build the line, showing something of the insular travelling and haulage conditions of the nineteenth century, the construction of the railway and the service it provided until the inevitable closure in the mid twentieth century. It does not cover the ill-fated Cromarty & Dingwall Light Railway, the story of which has been told elsewhere.

I am grateful to the staffs of the National Archives at Kew, the National Records of Scotland in Edinburgh, the Highland Archive in Inverness and the Groam House Museum at Rosemarkie, together with many individuals who have assisted me, particularly Richard Casserley and Hamish Stevenson for the photographs from their late fathers' magnificent collections and Godfrey Croughton for a selection of his tickets, as well as members of the Highland Railway Society. I have also been greatly helped by the many friends I have made since coming to live in the Black Isle. Finally my thanks are due to my wife Catherine for her encouragement and to Keith Fenwick for his help in preparing the text for publication.

Jack Kernahan
Wester Balmungie, Rosemarkie.

Fortrose station on 28th July 1913 looking towards Muir of Ord, with 'Small Ben' 4-4-0 no 4 Ben More pulling away from the turntable in the background. Luggage is being wheeled towards the guard's van. The lady may be the photographer's wife.   *(J B Sherlock)*

CHAPTER 1

LOCAL PROPOSALS

There was great excitement in the Black Isle in the autumn of 1889. At last it appeared that some attention was being paid to the requests from the Black Islanders that a railway be constructed in the peninsula, as at that time two railway companies, well known for their antagonism towards each other, were surveying the land and plotting the course for a line, each with a team of around forty on the ground. Starting at Muir of Ord, by the end of October they had passed Tore, Munlochy, Avoch and Fortrose and were bearing down on Cromarty. The companies were the Great North of Scotland Railway headquartered in Aberdeen and its Inverness based rival, the Highland Railway. But before looking at this sudden interest in bringing rail communication to the Black Isle it is necessary to look briefly at the history of these companies.

At the height of the 'Railway Mania', the Great North of Scotland Railway had been authorised on 26th June 1846 to build a line from Aberdeen to Inverness, but difficulties in raising the necessary capital resulted in a lengthy delay before the first section opened between Kittybrewster, on the northern outskirts of Aberdeen, and Huntly in September 1854. The continuation to Keith opened on 11th October 1856. Meanwhile, another company had started construction east from Inverness, the Inverness & Nairn Railway opening with great celebration on Monday 5th November 1855. The gap between Keith and Nairn was filled in stages by the Inverness & Aberdeen Junction Railway. With the opening of the bridge over the River Spey at Orton on 18th August 1858 through traffic commenced between the places in its title, and, although a change of stations was required in Aberdeen, through bookings became possible, for first class passengers at least, between Glasgow Queen Street and Inverness, and it was possible to travel by rail from Inverness to London. On 17th May 1861 the Inverness & Nairn Railway Company amalgamated with the Inverness & Aberdeen.

Within two months of this amalgamation, on 22nd July 1861, authority was granted for the construction of a much more direct line from Inverness to the south. This was the Inverness & Perth Junction Railway from Forres to join the existing line from Perth which had opened on 7th April 1856 between Dunkeld and Stanley Junction on the Scottish Midland Junction Railway (later Caledonian Railway), just over seven miles north of Perth. The first sod of this remarkable line over two major summits at Dava and Druimuachdar was cut on 17th October 1861 and the 104 miles opened to through traffic less than two years later, on 9th September 1863. The new route shortened the distance between Inverness and Perth by 54 miles and reduced the journey time substantially especially as it avoided the change of stations at Aberdeen. The Inverness & Perth and Inverness & Aberdeen Junction Railways amalgamated on 1st August 1865 as the Highland Railway Company. The Highland was determined to keep its eastern neighbour, the Great North of Scotland, out of its stronghold at Inverness. The Great North had been able to reach Elgin from Keith via Craigellachie since 1st July 1863, and a second route became possible with the completion of the route through the Moray coast villages in 1886.

Prior to the Great North's arrival in Elgin, the first stretch of line north of Inverness had been opened by the Inverness & Rossshire Railway which commenced traffic between Inverness and Dingwall on 11th June 1862. This line involved two major engineering works immediately after leaving the Highland capital, namely a masonry bridge over the River Ness and a swing bridge over the Caledonian Canal at Clachnaharry. Other major bridges were required to cross the rivers Beauly and Conon. The latter was a substantial masonry construction with skewed arches but the former was originally of wood, replaced in due course by steel spans. The line had been greatly supported by the Inverness & Aberdeen Junction, which formally took over the Rossshire company on 30th June 1862. From 1st August 1865, therefore, the line north from Inverness, which by that time had reached Bonar Bridge, became part of the Highland Railway. The first stations on the line between Inverness and Dingwall were at Bunchrew, Lentran, Beauly, Muir of Ord and Conon. Muir of Ord and Conon were ideally situated for the construction of branches into the Black Isle.

Although not, of course, an island, the Black Isle had relied more on the sea than the land for communication with a number of ferry routes north and south of the peninsula. The ferry routes from the south bank were across the narrowest portion of the Beauly Firth at Kessock and the mile long crossing between Chanonry Point and Fort George. This sometimes stormy crossing had existed from at least the fifteenth century, and at the beginning of the nineteenth century was one of the busiest ferries in the north of Scotland. At that time there had been no loss of life within mortal memory, but this record of safety came to an end in the early afternoon of Friday 15th November 1811 when the boat overturned some 600 yards out of Fort George in a strong southwest gale. The small boat had four boatmen, nine passengers and a pony on board. Only two passengers and the pony survived.

The Black Isle was one of the last districts in what were then known as the United Counties to have no public road transport. In June 1834 there was a proposal to run a one horse coach between Cromarty and Inverness, but a problem arose over the payment of mileage duty, the imposition of which would result in the fares being so high that the conveyance would be accessible only to the better off, while the poorer class who required it most would be unable to afford it. Two years later, during the summer months, an 'omnibus' ran every day except Sunday between Cromarty and Inverness passing through Chanonry, Rosemarkie and Avoch.

By the middle of the nineteenth century many Black Isle roads were described as 'miserably neglected' having been badly planned, although the Parliamentary roads from Rosemarkie leading towards Dingwall and Inverness and the turnpike road between Fort George ferry at Chanonry Point and Kessock ferry were kept in good repair. There was some improvement when a new low road was constructed between Cromarty and Munlochy. The previous higher level one was described as the most cheerless, uninviting and neglected in Scotland. In 1840 there were no mail or stage coaches passing through the parish of Rosemarkie. In 1854 a new road was constructed from Rosemarkie up the deep ravine known as Fairy Glen to Braelangwell. The work along the bank of the burn at Rosemarkie was difficult, involving cuttings through the rock up to 30ft in depth. When completed in the autumn of that year it became possible for a horse and gig to trot all the way from the Fort George ferry at Chanonry Point to the Invergordon ferry at Balblair, a route which until that time could be travelled over only at walking pace.

Great reliance was placed on shipping services. The steamers on the Moray Firth passed Chanonry Point weekly and delivered goods of all descriptions. They were well fitted out for passengers and plied to Aberdeen, Leith and London. Kenneth Mackenzie ran a small steamer

A view of Fortrose station showing a variety of five different types of coach making up the passenger train. In the background is Chanonry Point and the Moray Firth. (*John Alsop collection*)

named *Speedwell* between Fortrose and Inverness, but steamers carrying passengers could only enter and leave the harbour at Fortrose at high water. Salmon, packed in ice, was shipped to London as well as, in season, considerable quantities of pork and live pigs. The harbour at Avoch was well used, with coal being delivered from Newcastle (for sale in 1840 at 10d per hundredweight). Other imports were salt, lime and bone dust, while grain and wood were exported.

By 1865, as mentioned earlier, the railway system at Inverness was consolidated into one company, the Highland Railway, and a line passed the end of the Black Isle at Muir of Ord and Conon. It was therefore not unexpected that there would be a movement for a line to be built into the peninsula. A public meeting was held at the Caledonian Hotel in Inverness on Friday 14th July 1865, attended by a large number of interested parties including Provost Mackintosh, Bailie Watson, Rev Robert Young, Dr Mackenzie and Mr George Gillanders, Burgh Chamberlain, of Fortrose, plus Andrew Dougall, General Manager of what was within three weeks to become the Highland Railway, and Joseph Mitchell CE, the notable Forres born railway engineer who had designed all the existing lines in the Highlands. It was explained that establishing a railway from Muir of Ord station to Fortrose or Cromarty had long been contemplated, and the line had been partly surveyed and found to be one which would not entail great expense. Nearly all the land proprietors along the route were sympathetic. Mr Grigor of Elgin, solicitor and factor for Rosehaugh Estate, apologised for the absence of Mr James Fletcher of Rosehaugh who was ready to take fifty £10 shares, while the Burgh of Fortrose was prepared to take at least £1,000 of stock.

The intention was that Fortrose be the terminus meantime and details were given of the likely traffic, reflecting the trade carried on at that time. The merchandise delivered along the route amounted to nine loads per week. There were two boats plying regularly twice a week from Fortrose and Avoch to Inverness carrying goods and passengers. A two horse omnibus, generally well filled, ran twice a week between Kessock and Fortrose and the daily mail coach was often crowded with passengers. A large number of pigs, alive and dead, were sent across the Fort George ferry to be forwarded south from the station there and a great many were sent by the carriers to Muir of Ord station, while others were sent by boat from Avoch to Culloden station. (At that time the stations latterly known as Gollanfield and Allanfearn were named Fort George and Culloden respectively.) Other exports were ryegrass seed, barley and oats which were sent by steamer to Edinburgh. Sheep and lambs were sent to the London markets, while ten boats from Avoch went regularly to the haddock fishing. The bays of Fortrose and Rosemarkie abounded with herring of excellent quality during the winter months. Around £7,000 worth of potatoes were shipped annually to London from Fortrose harbour. A large number of turnips were grown on the Black Isle, and immense quantities of eggs were sent south every week. There were excellent freestone quarries along the route of the line, the stone being used in Inverness. The woollen factory at Avoch exported great quantities of goods to the south, the wool used being brought in from the south as well as all the materials required for the manufacturing process such as oils, dyestuffs and soaps. As well as all this potential goods traffic, the amenity of Fortrose with its fine air, seabathing and cheapness of living was likely to attract an increase in population as well as regular visitors.

The meeting accordingly approved a resolution 'that the formation of a railway from Muir of Ord to Fortrose was calculated to confer many benefits on the Black Isle and also to form an important feeder to the main line of railway and this meeting resolved to take all necessary steps to accomplish so desirable an undertaking'. A committee of 24, including representatives from Cromarty, Fortrose, Rosehaugh, Munlochy, Muir of Ord and Dingwall, was appointed, and the meeting authorised Messrs Mitchell & Co, engineers of Inverness, to examine the district and to make an interim survey of the line, with a probable estimate of the expense.

The fact that the proposed line was not to extend beyond Fortrose was a matter of concern to the inhabitants of Cromarty, and a public meeting was held there, in the Town Hall, on Monday 14th August to discuss what measures would be taken to have railway communication extended to the village. A 'large and influential' committee was appointed to promote the undertaking by procuring reliable information as to the extent of the traffic to be expected from the district and the amount of shares which could be subscribed for. The route suggested for the line was through the valley of Raddery, continuing through Glen Urquhart to a terminus in Cromarty, this being the shortest, cheapest and most beautiful. On 26th August both committees met and agreed to act in concert as the only means of obtaining a railway to either Fortrose or Cromarty and asked Messrs Mitchell to prepare an estimate to extend the line beyond Fortrose to Cromarty.

On 22nd August, just five weeks after they had been instructed, Messrs Mitchell forwarded to Mr Grigor in Elgin the plan, section and report, over which they indicated that they had taken great pains, being anxious to ascertain at how cheap a rate they could really make a road-side railway. In the letter accompanying the plan, Joseph Mitchell stated that if the line stopped at Avoch it could be very much cheaper, because going on to Fortrose involved construction over the steep cliff between the villages. The cost of the line simply to Avoch would amount to £41,769 exclusive of land, compared with £56,000 for the complete line to Fortrose. He clearly doubted that the full amount could be raised but suggested promoting the whole line and then scaling it back to Avoch if the funds raised were insufficient.

The following day, 23rd August, a further letter was received by Mr Grigor from Mitchells. This referred to the possible continuation of the line to Cromarty. The engineers suggested that the line would need to run along the foot of the arable land of Mountpleasant and terminate at a field at the top of the high terrace where the public road from the west end of Fortrose

> Engineer's Chambers
> Inverness 22nd Augt 1865
>
> My dear Sir
>
> I now send you the Plan, Sections and Report on the Black Isle Railway, with which we have taken great pains, for I was anxious to ascertain at how cheap a rate we could really make a Road-side Railway, and you will notice the result of our examination & Calculations.
>
> Of course if you stopped at Avoch the Line would be very much cheaper, because going on to Fortrose involves the construction of the Line across that steep cliff. The cost of the Line simply to Avoch would amount to £41,679 exclusive of Land, but it might be inexpedient as well as unpopular, in the first instance, to allude to making Avoch the Terminus, until funds should fail for making the whole.
>
> As you request we have given you the amount in value of the Land which will be required from each Proprietor. My belief is it is a full value, but it is possible some may be a little more & some less.
>
> Wm Grigor, Esq   Yours very faithfully
> Writer, Elgin   (Signed J Mitchell)

joined the old Dingwall road. This would make the station at Fortrose 202 feet above sea level, 136 feet higher than the site proposed for a line terminating in the town centre as contained in the plans submitted the previous day. By locating the station at the higher level, it would be possible to continue the line to Cromarty by way of Ryeflat, Whitebog and over the 490 feet summit at Mulbuie. However, as levels had not been taken, the engineers were uncertain at that stage as to the nature of the ground and the gradients involved. Joseph Mitchell continued that he was decidedly of the opinion that the line to Cromarty should embrace the villages of Munlochy and Avoch as well as the burghs of Fortrose and Rosemarkie, since although the extension to Cromarty necessarily required the line to be kept high up on the hill at Fortrose, a station there on the high terrace, there being no intermediate terrace between that and the lower part of the field, would be available to Rosemarkie as well as Fortrose. The line proposed by the valley of Raddery and the crossroads two or three miles from Fortrose was, in the opinion of Mitchell, too distant from Avoch or Fortrose to be of service and they could not see any way in which any line which did not come close to Avoch, Fortrose or Rosemarkie could remunerate the shareholders or accommodate the public.

A meeting of the original committee was held on Tuesday 29th August in the Caledonian Hotel to report on progress. No mention was made of the suggested higher level line which would have permitted an extension to Cromarty. The plans prepared for the line terminating at the lower level in Fortrose were presented by William Paterson CE of Messrs Mitchell & Co and these were examined with great interest. The recommended route from Muir of Ord was to pass south of Kilcoy Castle and the Free Church manse where it would cross the road from Tarradale to Tore, and then cross the Tore to Kessock road at a point 660 yards south of the inn. Thence the line would proceed to Munlochy, crossing the burn at a point 200 yards above the village, where the existing road would be diverted and Munlochy station situated. The line was then to keep to the south side of the road which would be crossed at Muirale-House, then crossing over the Avoch burn, passing to the north of the Established Church at Avoch and continuing to a terminus in the flat part of the field above the old distillery at the west end of Fortrose, which was described as 'admirably adapted for a station'. The estimated cost of the works was £56,000, which included seventeen bridges over roads and nine bridges over streams plus four stations. The estimated cost including the land and other claims was £61,684, which was £4,673 per mile. Messrs Mitchell felt assured that the railway could be satisfactorily executed for this sum. No mention was made of the much reduced cost for a line terminating at Avoch. During the meeting a telegram was received from Mr Mackenzie of Avoch indicating that he would take £2,000 of stock, and Mr Mackenzie of Allangrange stated that he would take £500 and seek also to take stock in respect of the value of his land to be used for the line. Mr Fletcher of Rosehaugh confirmed that he too would add the value of his land, estimated at £1,000, to the £5,000 he had already subscribed. Various other sums were subscribed at the meeting giving a total of upwards of £18,000. Another committee was appointed to canvass Inverness and the neighbourhood for additional financial support. A further meeting was planned for Friday 22nd September by which time the detailed plans of the line to Cromarty were anticipated to be available, and all attending were enjoined to use all diligence in the meantime to increase the subscription list.

The meeting on 22nd September was well attended and Mr Grigor, factor for Rosehaugh Estate, read a letter from Messrs Mitchell in which they confirmed that, as requested, they had made a survey of the suggested line from Munlochy, through the Raddery valley, to Cromarty. They reported that on the approach to Cromarty the ground was very steep and it had been suggested that the line would have to terminate at Newton, about a mile and a quarter from the town. Messrs Mitchell thought that this would be a great inconvenience and that notwithstanding the steepness the line should be carried down to the town, if not to the harbour. In the meantime, however, they had surveyed only as far as Newton, to a point suggested by Colonel Ross. The engineers had looked also at constructing a line which would extend the proposed line to Fortrose by way of the Rosemarkie burn and onwards to Cromarty. The works required for any line in this direction would be of so formidable a character, involving a large viaduct over the Rosemarkie Valley 110 ft in height and a gradient of 1 in 50, that the expense involved would be wholly disproportionate to the value of any amount of traffic likely to be carried on it. They were therefore of the opinion that any line to Cromarty from Muir of Ord would have to leave the Fortrose line at Munlochy and run through the Raddery valley. The cost of a line using this route, for the complete section from Muir of Ord to Newton, a distance of 19½ miles, would be £83,120, inclusive of the cost of land.

Subscriptions had been disappointing. The £18,000 mentioned at the previous meeting had included an anticipated £3,000 from the Dingwall and Muir of Ord districts. The amount actually promised was only £250. Major James Wardlaw of Balmaduthy, the Chairman, said that he had no doubt that subscribers would become more liberal if it was determined where the railway was to go, whether by the coast to Fortrose or by the high level route to Cromarty. Mr Grigor was of the opinion that they could not proceed until they knew how much might be raised in the Cromarty area, given the substantial extra cost of taking the line there. Provost Ross of Cromarty then produced the Cromarty list, showing a total of £7,000, but he considered that more could be raised if it was settled that the line was to go through Raddery, as if it were otherwise it would be more convenient for the Cromarty folk for the line to join the main line at Conon.

There was deep concern at the amount which had been raised, and Mr Grigor confirmed that it was necessary to have raised two-thirds of the cost before taking the plans to Parliament.

A decision had to be made within the next few weeks to seek Parliamentary permission in the next session, bearing in mind the time required to prepare the necessary plans. Discussion continued on the merits of all three routes. To applause the Chairman stated that the original promoters and supporters had regarded it as a *sine qua non* that the line would go to Fortrose and Rosemarkie. To go via the Raddery valley would place Fortrose three miles from the nearest station and cut out Avoch altogether. Mr Fletcher considered that the only chance of the railway ever proving remunerative was by taking the low level line to Fortrose. A motion to the effect that this route be adopted was put to the meeting. Provost Ross said that, having sensed the feeling of the meeting, he would not waste time by moving an amendment, but should the motion be carried he begged leave to withdraw the list of Cromarty subscribers. The committee was reappointed to seek further subscriptions in order that sufficient might be raised to take the scheme to Parliament. As the subscription list totalled only £20,000 and an approach to the Highland Railway for support proved fruitless, nothing further came of this first proposal for a Black Isle railway.

The Black Islanders did not let the matter rest for long. Early in 1872, after canvassing in the district, three memorials were prepared by the landowners, farmers and other residents praying that the Highland Railway would either construct a railway from Muir of Ord to Fortrose or render assistance to local parties in the event that the company itself was unable to carry through the undertaking. On 2nd April a deputation, comprising Mr James Cameron of Balnakyle, Mr Peter Grant the bank agent at Fortrose, and Rev John Gibson minister of the Established Church at Avoch, was received at a meeting of the board of directors of the Highland Railway in connection with the memorials. The Chairman informed them that the Highland Company would not undertake the construction of the line but would be prepared to work it on reasonable terms, while as regards pecuniary assistance the Board could not give any opinion without having an opportunity of consulting the shareholders. The deputation undertook to furnish a list of the subscribers together with a survey and estimate of the expense and a statement of the probable traffic. The folk of Cromarty were not far behind! On 24th April the Highland board received a petition from Colonel Ross of Cromarty, signed by the inhabitants of the parishes of Cromarty and Resolis on the north coast of the Black Isle, regarding the projected line. The Secretary was instructed to give Colonel Ross a similar response to that given to the deputation received earlier in the month.

William Grigor, the solicitor from Elgin who had advised in the earlier attempt to construct the line, was heavily involved in the new scheme. Colonel Ross, Mr James Fletcher of Rosehaugh and Mr Grigor met in London with His Grace the Duke of Sutherland and John Pender, Member of Parliament for the Wick District of Burghs, which included Cromarty, Dingwall and Dornoch. At that meeting the Duke and Mr Pender recommended that the promoters consider using the narrow gauge in an effort to reduce costs. Mr Grigor continued in correspondence with Andrew Dougall, general manager and secretary of the Highland Railway. Mr Dougall was sympathetic and wrote to Mr Grigor on 15th June suggesting that Mr Gillanders, now Inspector of Poor at the Black Isle Combination Poor House, which had opened in 1859, would be a suitable person to make a report on the potential traffic. George Gillanders would, of course, already be known to Mr Grigor as he had been involved in the 1865 proposal when he was Burgh Chamberlain of Fortrose, a post from which he had resigned on 2nd November 1868. Dougall added an interesting postscript to his letter: "I hope you will keep clear of the narrow gauge. AD". Sadly William Grigor died, aged 68, a few months later, on 8th September. A bachelor who had suffered illness for the last twenty years, he was

Part of the Moray Firth viewed from Balmungie, two miles north of Rosemarkie, showing Fort George to the left on the distant shore and Chanonry Point on the right. (*Jack Kernahan*)

devoted to his profession, and was described by Mr Fletcher of Rosehaugh, whose factor he was, as a man whose energy and sagacity and admirable business talents made him a valuable counsellor and a powerful ally.

James Cameron and George Gillanders spent the summer of 1872 visiting all the resident proprietors and tenants paying £40 of rental and upwards in the Black Isle to collect information and particulars of probable traffic. They suggested that the line run from Muir of Ord through Redcastle, past Tore Inn, Munlochy and Avoch to Fortrose, thence running north to Mounthigh and then turning east by Poyntsfield and Davidston to Cromarty. Stations were proposed at Tore Inn, Munlochy, Avoch, Fortrose, Poyntzfield and Cromarty. Such a line, about twenty miles in length, was not expected to present any engineering difficulties. Their report on possible traffic was similar to that of seven years previously. Large traffic was expected in cattle, sheep and pigs as well as in hay, grain, ryegrass, seeds and artificial manures. Large cargoes of guano, upwards of 1,500 tons, for Morayshire and Banffshire farmers arrived annually at Cromarty and would be sent by railway instead of being despatched by sea in small cargoes as at present. A good deal of lime and coal used in the district would come by rail and there would be a large export traffic of stones from the freestone quarries along the line. Export of fish would also be important. Herrings and sprat were landed at Cromarty and Avoch, salmon was caught at several places along the coast, while oysters and other shellfish were caught at Avoch and Rosemarkie.

Passenger traffic estimates were prepared by Andrew Dougall of the Highland Railway, having regard to the population of the Black Isle in comparison with other districts of similar character and nature in possession of railway accommodation. Based on a line twenty miles in length he computed that in the months of July to September £5 per mile per week would be earned. In April, May, June and October this would be £3.10/- per week, reducing to £2.10/- in the other five months. The annual total expected income from passengers was £3,600. Goods and livestock were carefully calculated to bring in £3,818.15.8d while carrying mails would earn £150, a grand total of £7,568.15.8d The population served was 11,180.

On Thursday 24th October a notice was published by Mr Fletcher calling a meeting to be held the following day at 1 pm in the Royal Hotel, Fortrose, of the promoters and all others interested in the projected railway to Cromarty. Thirty nine gentlemen attended, including five ministers and the provosts of Fortrose and Dingwall. James Fletcher was elected chairman. He reviewed the history of the 1865 proposal, reading the letter from Messrs Mitchell & Co dated 23rd August 1865 which had stressed the desirability of incorporating Avoch and Fortrose in the line to Cromarty rather than going through the Raddery valley and running via a high level through Fortrose where the station site was approximately 200 feet above sea level. He indicated that there had been 'a want of earnestness and faith in the project'. There had been conflicting interests between the districts and only £18,000 to £20,000 of the required £80,000 to £100,000 had been subscribed. There had also been a failure to enlist the support of others beyond the district who might have been expected to assist. At that time the Dingwall & Skye Railway and the Sutherland Railway had been in progress and of more interest than the Black Isle. These lines were now complete and in full operation and traffic on the Highland line had increased beyond the most optimistic speculations of its most enthusiastic supporters. Despite the recommendation of His Grace the Duke of Sutherland, Mr Fletcher was now strongly of the opinion that the line should be of the same gauge as the Highland Railway, not the narrow gauge. The intended line would keep to the high level behind Fortrose, continuing by Ryefleet and Whitebog and across the summit to Cromarty. He considered that this was preferable to going through Mounthigh as was suggested by Messrs Cameron and Gillanders.

The projected revenue figures were then revealed. Mr Fletcher stressed the credentials of Messrs Cameron and Gillanders as being perfectly qualified from their local knowledge and business talents to produce reliable statistics. The figures had not been 'got up to mislead the public', nor had they been 'cooked' or 'doctored' to suit a purpose, as those attending would be aware had been done in other cases. In the last seven years great improvements had been made in the Black Isle including a large expenditure in both money and labour. Direct communication with the great centres of trade and commerce was essential in order that the capital and enterprise of the agricultural population might have a fair chance of competing with other districts. He was sanguine regarding the future profitability of the line and, to applause, advised those present to immediately put down their names for shares, fully expecting that the shares might even come to a premium before construction was complete. The line had been surveyed to Fortrose and this would be continued to Cromarty if circumstances justified it. The total cost was expected to be around £60,000 for the line as far as Fortrose, excluding plant which would be furnished by the Highland Railway. By the close of the meeting £20,000 had been subscribed by twenty three of those attending. A provisional committee was formed to continue the project. This comprised forty nine gentlemen, including the Duke of Sutherland, three Members of Parliament, among them Alexander Matheson, Chairman of the Highland Railway, as well as Colonel Ross of Cromarty and James Fletcher of Rosehaugh. Appointments for an intended company were made. Martin and Leslie were to be appointed Parliamentary Agents, Murdoch Paterson CE the engineer, and Grigor and Young, Elgin, solicitors. The Caledonian Bank and the Commercial Bank of Scotland were to be bankers while Andrew Dougall, General Manager and Secretary of the Highland Railway was to be interim secretary. It was stressed that the appointment of the professional gentlemen was made on the express understanding that they should look to the undertaking itself for their remuneration and not to the committee as individuals.

The next meeting of the provisional committee was held on Saturday 2nd November.

A view of Fortrose from the west showing the recently constructed railway in the foreground, part of the lengthy pier which extended from the harbour and from which steamers sailed to Inverness, and, in the background, Chanonry Point and Fort George.   *(Author's collection)*

Mr Fletcher was unable to be present so the Chair was taken by Colonel Ross, who read a letter to be sent to Mr Fletcher in which he stated that in addition to the £5,000 subscribed by himself (Colonel Ross) and the amounts already indicated as forthcoming from the others in the Cromarty area at the previous meeting he would undertake to procure a further £2,000 from the people of Cromarty. The Duke of Sutherland, as Lord Lieutenant of Cromarty, had indicated that he would subscribe £2,000. The letter stated that the Colonel was willing to give this undertaking if Mr Fletcher would undertake with the aid of the other five parishes to double his original promise of £10,000, this to exclude any contributions forthcoming from the Burghs of Fortrose and Cromarty. Time for raising the funds was becoming crucial. A notice had to be advertised in a newspaper published in the county for three consecutive weeks in the month of November, the surveys had to be completed and a book of reference made up and lodged by the end of the month. The meeting was adjourned until the following Wednesday, during which time further canvassing for funds was to be undertaken.

Twenty five gentlemen attended the reconvened meeting on 6th November, Colonel Ross again taking the Chair. He reported that Mr Fletcher had declined the proposal put to him in the letter sent after the previous meeting, but had sent a subsequent telegram in which he said he would take stock to the value of £15,000, including the value of the land belonging to him through which the line would pass. The canvassing had produced a further £3,975, the largest contributions totalling £1,445 coming from Cromarty. The total now raised was £31,010. As this sum was insufficient to warrant the committee applying to Parliament in the current session the meeting was adjourned until 9th December, 1872. All those present pledged themselves to use every effort to obtain further subscriptions. No meeting took place on 9th December. It was 'postponed until further notice'. Nothing further happened in respect of this second attempt by the folk of the Black Isle to have their railway.

CHAPTER 2

RIVAL SCHEMES

For the next eighteen years the Black Isle thought no more about having a railway; Fortrose decided to develop its harbour and look to the sea for its transport links. A petition had first been made in 1813 to the Commissioners for Highland Roads and Bridges for support for a harbour, which was completed by Thomas Telford at a cost of £4,000 in 1817. In 1878, six years after the collapse of local attempts to build a railway, the Town Council obtained authority to construct a 230 yard long wooden landing pier, attached to the harbour. This was completed in 1882 when the Black Isle Steam Shipping Company started a ferry service to Inverness. In 1883 the *Annie*, a schooner of 116 tons, 84 feet in length, was built by Geddie Shipyards at Kingston and Garmouth at the mouth of the River Spey and this operated between its home port of Fortrose and Inverness under the ownership of John Henderson. The skipper was Donald Paterson.

Henderson was manager and a director of the company, but the chairman was James Douglas Fletcher, son of James Fletcher who had been a driving force behind the earlier schemes for a railway. A second hand steamer, appropriately renamed *Rosehaugh* and commanded by Captain Grieve, was also placed on the crossing of the Moray Firth, or, as that part of it was occasionally described at that time, the Firth of Inverness. Montford Baddeley, a distinguished guide book writer, described the crossing in his 1884 publication :

A good steamer has been put on to this route and those who enjoy a pleasant sail in calm water and amid beautiful scenery will not repent of devoting a few hours to the excursion. Passengers are allowed about three hours at Fortrose.

There were no further thoughts in the Black Isle about a railway until 11th October 1889 when James Douglas Fletcher, who had inherited Rosehaugh on the death of his father in 1885, received an unexpected visit from the manager and engineer of the Great North of Scotland Railway Company, who informed him of the intentions of their company to construct a railway through the district. That evening Mr Fletcher was speaking at a public banquet in Inverness given to the Lord Advocate. He mentioned the totally unexpected Great North interest in the Black Isle to directors of the Highland Railway present at the function. Within a few days the Highland engineers were busy surveying the ground for a competing line from Muir of Ord to Fortrose! The Black Isle had afforded a field to the Highland for a display of enterprise ever since the opening of the Ross-shire line in 1862, but they had never asked Parliament for powers to open up the district until they heard of the Great North's intentions. What then had prompted this interest in constructing a railway in the Black Isle from such an unlikely source?

It will be remembered that the original intention of the Great North of Scotland Railway had been to build a line between Aberdeen and Inverness, but lack of funds and the local endeavours of the Invernessians led to the route being served by the Great North east of Keith and the Highland west of Elgin, with both companies having routes between Keith and Elgin. In 1885 the Great North applied to the Board of Trade to compel the Highland to run two trains a day connecting with their trains at Elgin, but the Railway Commissioners fixed Keith as the exchange point. They described the Highland's breaking of connections as 'one of the most vexatious things they had seen in railway working'. The following year the General Managers of both companies made a truce, to last seven years, this agreement including through workings and timetabled connections.

Before the truce was under way, the Great North complained that the Highland was sending traffic from Inverness consigned via Aberdeen by way of Dunkeld. In 1886 the Great North intimated 91 breaches and the Highland 590, of which arbitrators allowed only 13. The Great North decided to build its own line from Elgin to Inverness, running south from Elgin through Pluscarden, via Forres and Nairn, but with a short branch onto a pier to be constructed near Campbelltown, from which a steam ferry was to be operated across the Moray Firth to Fortrose. A railway was to run through the Black Isle from Fortrose to join the Highland Railway at Muir of Ord, where running powers over the existing Highland line to Inverness were required. At the same time powers were sought for a line from Elgin to the Moray Firth coastal villages at Hopeman and Burghead. In addition to visiting Mr Fletcher, the deputation of directors and officials of the Great North visited several districts in the Black Isle as far as Cromarty and the agriculturists of the district suggested that Mr Fletcher should go to Aberdeen to have a formal meeting with the Great North directors. There was unanimous support for the new railway throughout the Black Isle, as the Highland had for some twenty five years ignored the district.

In the autumn of 1889 there were proposals for an amalgamation of the two companies. On 6th November the Great North board passed a resolution to the effect that if the Highland Railway did not consent to the joint notice for amalgamation they gave notice of their intentions to proceed with their proposed lines to Inverness, the Black Isle and Burghead. The amalgamation failed. If it had gone ahead, it is unlikely that the Black Isle would have had its railway.

A meeting of shareholders of the Highland Railway was held on Tuesday 29th October where the proposed Great North scheme was described as 'perfectly unnecessary and uncalled for'. The company resolved to give the proposals the most strenuous opposition and proposed their own line through the Black Isle. The Chairman's words were:

> *Should we succeed in opposing the Great North of Scotland Railway, or should they abandon their scheme, it will be a question for the company to decide whether this is a proper time for a line of that kind, but it will be a very good line to make and at some other time we will, no doubt, make it.*

Local feeling was that if the Great North failed there would be no railway, although the Highland had admitted that it was a good line to make and would be likely to pay. The Black Isle folk were encouraged to support the Great North and put no faith in the false promises and surveys of the Highland.

The following Wednesday a meeting of the proprietors and farmers from the east side of the Black Isle and the inhabitants of Cromarty was held in the Victoria Hall, Cromarty to consider the current movement for the construction of a railway. The question of the possible amalgamation of the two companies was considered, and it was hoped that there would be no amalgamation. To great applause a motion seeking a railway to Cromarty was passed. A second motion was put merely observing with satisfaction the recent statement by the

Chairman of the Highland Railway to the effect that in his opinion a railway through the Black Isle would be profitable, while a third motion merely stated that any railway, to be successful, must be so constructed as to have a siding in the harbour of Cromarty, described as "the best natural harbour in the world." A suggestion was made that an approach be made to the West Highland Railway, at that time just commencing operations for the construction of the line from Craigendoran to Fort William! The difficulties which beset Cromarty fishermen in being so far from a railway were stressed. At that time they could only go to sea for three days a week, having to take their catch to Invergordon where they would often miss the train connection to the southern markets. A railway to transport their catches would allow them to be at sea every day. Mr Skinner, the local fish curer, confirmed that a higher price would be achieved for the fish, for the benefit of all, fishing being the only industry in the Burgh of Cromarty. Tourism was also stressed, as there was a great demand for pleasure and health resorts. A railway could make Cromarty, rather than Nairn, the Brighton of the north. Mr Thomson of the Caledonian Bank dampened enthusiasm somewhat when he told the meeting that one of the surveyors he had met recently at Fortrose had told him that it was unlikely that the railway would go to Cromarty at present on account of seeming carelessness on the part of agriculturists as to whether it was constructed or not. Those present considered that there was no truth in this idea and that there should be a combined effort to get a railway. Eventually it was decided to elect a deputation to lay before the Highland and Great North companies the views of the meeting.

The Black Isle folk continued to be sceptical about the Highland's proposals. There was an opinion that 'the Highland were very good at surveying, but they never get any further. Though they got a Bill to construct a line in the Black Isle, if the Great North of Scotland retire the probability is that it could be the Day of Judgement before Cromarty or Jemimaville could thank the Highland Railway Company'. Opinion was decidedly in favour of the Great North, word being that they were planning to build a circular line, running from Muir of Ord to Fortrose, then skirting the eastern slope and wheeling round to Cromarty. The line would then continue via Jemimaville round the western side until it reached Muir of Ord again.

There was not long to wait until the intentions of the railway companies became public as details of the lines for which Bills were to be sought in the 1890 Parliamentary Session were promulgated in the middle of November. Three lines were detailed in the *Rossshire Journal* dated 22nd November. One was the Garve & Ullapool, but the other two were the rival schemes for the Black Isle. The Great North of Scotland Railway proposed a line from the existing Highland line at Muir of Ord to Fortrose, including the acquisition of the pier at Fortrose Harbour which they intended to extend and from which operate a steam ferry crossing the Moray Firth to a new pier which they planned to build at the end of a short spur from their proposed line from Elgin to Inverness near Treeton, about half a mile south of Campbelltown. The Highland's line was also to run from Muir of Ord over roughly the same course as their rival's to Fortrose, but was to continue via Rosemarkie where it would make a ninety degree turn to the south east terminating at Chanonry Point. Also proposed was a line from Fort George station on the existing line between Inverness and Nairn to Fort George itself, a distance of just over 3 miles 3 chains. The two proposed Highland lines terminated at the points between which there was the long established ferry service.

The proposed routes were very similar between Muir of Ord and Avoch. The Great North would initially run south of the Highland's route to near Kilcoy, from which point it would be to the north, going closer to Tore. Between Munlochy and Avoch the Great North would pass through Rosehaugh Estate, which the Highland would avoid by taking the line to the south of the road between the villages. The main difference was between Avoch and Fortrose. The Highland, intending to continue to Rosemarkie, was to take the higher route through Craig Wood as the earlier local proposals would have done, but the Great North was to cross the road at the east end of Avoch and follow the shore from there to terminate at Fortrose Harbour.

There was no mention of Cromarty and the eastern districts of the Black Isle in either company's scheme. This brought dismay to the people there and immediately, on Monday 18th November, a deputation of gentlemen from Cromarty proceeded to Inverness for a meeting with Andrew Dougall, general manager of the Highland Railway, prior to going on to Aberdeen to meet with the directors of the Great North. It was, of course, impossible for the schemes which were to be put forward to that Parliamentary Session to be altered, but the Cromarty men decided that their agitation for a railway would continue. During December the all engrossing subject for discussion in Cromarty was the railway. With what was contended to be the finest crops in Scotland produced from the fertile soil of the area, the finest natural harbour in the world and the finest bathing beach in Scotland, the people of the area were very keen that the Great North should continue their line to the burgh. They did not want the Highland. "We are afraid they would be too Highland for us, as they have in many cases been for themselves!"

On Friday 13th December the Great North directors met Fortrose Town Council, with a deputation also present from Cromarty and other parts of the Black Isle. While unqualified support was given to the Great North, doubt was expressed as to whether they were in earnest. The directors explained their proposals, which included taking over the harbour at Fortrose from the Town Council and enlarging it by extending the already lengthy pier into deeper water so that large steamers could call. The 230 yard pier was to be extended by approximately

An early depiction of the ferry between Fort George and Chanonry Point which operated until the 1930s. The Highland Railway originally indicated that it would develop this crossing, but nothing came of their pledge to do so.   *(Courtesy Margaret Tanner)*

80 yards, making it just under a fifth of a mile in length! They then proceeded to Campbelltown where they explained their proposals for the construction of a pier and were met with similar enthusiasm to that shown at Fortrose. Fortrose Town Council decided to dissent from the Highland Railway bill as their proposed route would divert traffic from the harbour there and be a serious loss to the burgh. Public opinion in the Black Isle continued to be in favour of the Great North. A large and enthusiastic public meeting of the inhabitants of Fortrose and the eastern portion of the area was held in the Fortrose Town Hall on 23rd January 1890 to consider the rival schemes. James Douglas Fletcher took the chair at what was the largest public meeting he had ever attended in the town. The unquestionable feeling in the district was that the Great North scheme was finished and complete, while the Highland had no intention of actually building the line, which was merely a device to prevent the Great North moving into the district. It was noted that passenger traffic had been gradually increasing for the last 15 to 20 years, chiefly owing to the facilities afforded by the steamers plying between Fortrose and Inverness. It often cost a third class passenger more in hires, ferries and cabs to get to Inverness from the Black Isle than it did for him to travel from Inverness to Glasgow or Edinburgh. The vote was unanimously in favour of the Great North, although it had no plans to go beyond Fortrose. An attraction was the proposed steamer service to the new pier to be built south of Campbelltown. Unlike other Scottish railways, the Great North had no experience of operating ships. The Caledonian had recently formed their own Steam Packet Company to operate on the Firth of Clyde, where the North British were also entrenched, having started their steamer operations in England, at Silloth in 1862. The Glasgow & South Western followed on the Clyde in 1891, while the Highland had already given up shipping following withdrawal from the routes to Orkney from Scrabster in 1882. Possibly their experience was such that their plans involved building railways to both sides of the Fort George ferry, but not taking on the ferry itself.

The Fort George ferry was still operated by an open boat, always stationed at the Chanonry Point side, where there was a jetty. There was no pier at Fort George, where landing was on the stone and shingle beach. Passengers arriving at Fort George had to signal across to the ferryman, using a wooden signal which could be raised when the ferry was required. At night passengers had to go into the fort, beg to borrow a lantern and flash it from the ramparts in the hope that it might be seen! In fog or falling snow signals could not be seen. In winter the mile long crossing could take up to two hours, especially when the wind was from the southwest or northwest. When gales blew the only place to land passengers and goods was to the east side of the fort. Walking on the beach was difficult, with the distance to the entrance of the fort being at least quarter of a mile. No carts or vehicles of any sort could cross the ground.

The Great North was intent on taking over and extending the pier at Fortrose. However feeling in the town was strongly opposed to this, as they would lose local control of their harbour. At the meeting on 13th December mentioned above the Great North directors had suggested that they would take over the pier and harbour in exchange merely for assuming all the liabilities and obligations of the Harbour Trustees. In other words, no cash would pass hands. The Trustees countered this by desiring that the Great North make an alternative offer under which the control and administration of the pier would remain with, and be vested in, the Harbour Trustees and their employees, subject that due accommodation should be made for the railway company's traffic, it being agreed that such traffic was not to be conducted in such a way as to interfere with or injure any other traffic which may come to the pier and harbour. The railway company would pay an annual sum in consideration of wayleave.

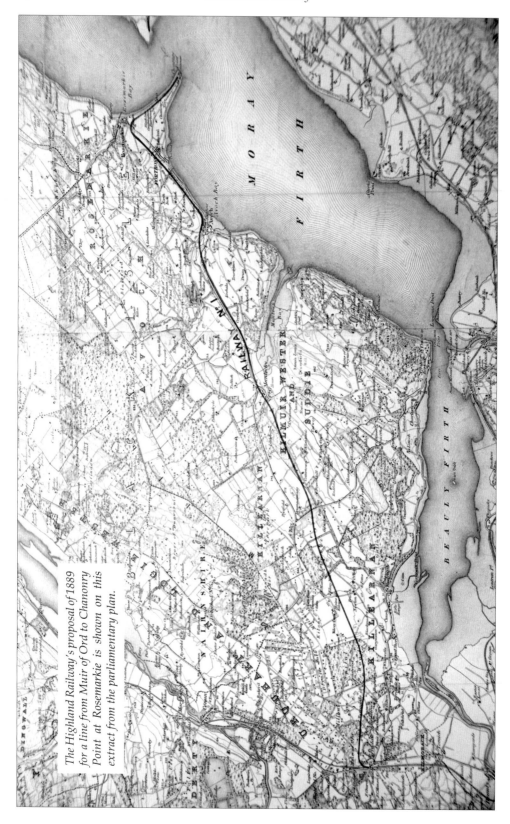

The Highland Railway's proposal of 1889 for a line from Muir of Ord to Chanonry Point at Rosemarkie is shown on this extract from the parliamentary plan.

Another alternative put forward was that the railway company should take over the wooden pier, its revenues, liabilities and obligations and the Harbour would continue to be under the control and administration of the Trustees, who would exact all tolls applicable to it. The Town Clerk, John Henderson, in communicating these ideas to the Great North, stated that personally he did not think that the last proposal was a desirable arrangement as it could scarcely fail to result in future trouble.

Despite this the Great North got its own way, and on 23rd January 1890 the agreement that the Great North take over the harbour was approved by Fortrose Town Council and a resolution passed that the meeting of the Town Council, acting also as Harbour Trustees and Police Commissioners, approved of the Great North of Scotland (Various Powers) Bill presently pending in Parliament and disapproved of the Highland Railway (New Lines) Bill. A further resolution was passed to petition Parliament in favour of the Great North and against the Highland. The formal agreement regarding the harbour was signed on 19th February and countersigned by the Great North directors a week later.

Cromarty was still not giving up. After the Great North directors had met with the members of Fortrose Town Council on 13th December, they received a deputation from Cromarty who pointed out that for a Black Isle railway to be successful and beneficial to the district it must run along the north side to Cromarty. The directors seemed to be favourably impressed and arranged for their agent to visit the town to collect evidence and information in regard to the resources and requirements of the district. They departed in the knowledge that they would probably be unanimously supported in the town and surrounding district. The Black Islanders were certainly impressed. Comment was made: "If the Highland Company would treat their customers, and even their best servants, with more consideration, no other company would compete with them north of Inverness. Let the Great North push on and they are sure to

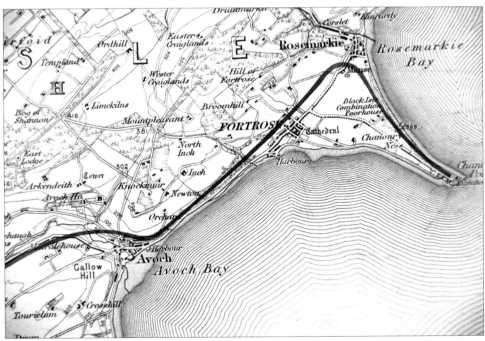

Detail from the 1889 Highland Railway parliamentary plan showing the route from Avoch to their terminus.

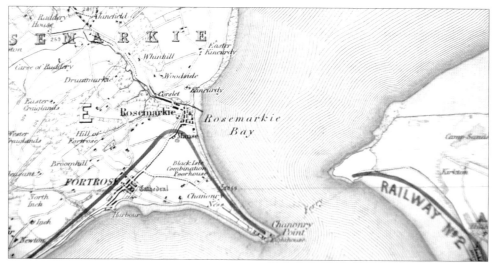

The Highland Railway's proposed routes to Chanonry Point and to Fort George, between which points a ferry had operated for centuries (see pages 8 and 20).

augment their revenue and benefit the public." The desire for railways in Easter Ross was not restricted to the Black Isle. That same night a meeting was held in Portmahomack seeking a line from Fearn or Tain.

The Great North continued to solicit support. A largely attended meeting was held in the Drill Hall at Munlochy on Saturday 15th February to consider the proposals of both companies. A statement from the Highland was produced indicating that the company would not make a railway through the Black Isle unless forced to do so. On the other hand they had the assurance

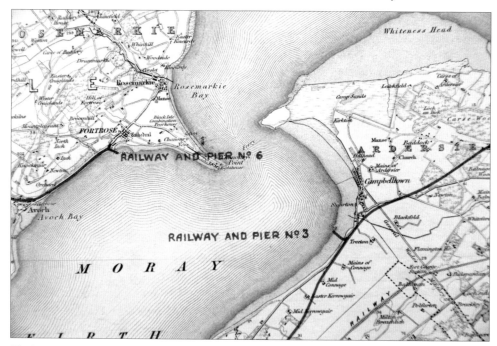

The locations of the steamer piers for the Great North of Scotland Railway's proposal are shown on this extract from their parliamentary plans.

from the Great North that they would build the line if they got their Bill and the Chairman of the meeting, Colonel A P Smith, thought it was their duty as well as in their interest to support the Great North. To frequent applause Mr Charles Innes, the Inverness solicitor for the Great North, explained very fully the proposals of the two companies, and a petition was drawn up and signed by all present in favour of the Great North and against the Highland.

Not all were in favour of the Great North. The minister of the Established Church at Avoch, Rev John Gibson, who had been actively involved in the attempt to have a railway built in 1872, was strongly opposed to the line, but only because of its proposed route through Church lands. The line as laid out would pass within 45 yards of the front of his manse, where he lived with his wife, cook, housemaid and under-housemaid. Indeed the limit of deviation came up to his front door. The railway was also to pass through his glebe and bisect his garden. He maintained that if the railway was built as intended the manse would be rendered practically uninhabitable, the garden destroyed and the glebe greatly deteriorated in value. The access road to the manse would be stopped up and the whole construction would be extremely injurious to him as incumbent of the parish and his successors. He maintained that the Highland Railway's proposals, going through to Rosemarkie and Chanonry Point would serve the whole area much better than the Great North of Scotland line, which did not connect at any point with their existing system. The minister's petition also pointed out that if the Great North Bill was passed the company was not in a financial position to build all the proposed lines, estimated to cost about £750,000, which he believed the company would be unable to raise. He had also been advised, and accordingly alleged, that the railway was badly designed in its engineering details. During March, Mr Blyth, engineer for the Great North, met Rev Gibson, who indicated that he was willing to withdraw his petition if the company would buy his manse, a very substantial and well appointed building, at arbitration value. This was reported to the directors who deferred consideration of the matter and nothing further was heard of it.

Some hope for Cromarty was forthcoming when in March the Highland engineers undertook a survey of a proposed extension from Rosemarkie to Cromarty. The difficulty in passing up the ravine at Rosemarkie, Fairy Glen, had been overcome, and draft plans showed that the line could be constructed without any great engineering difficulty or expense. The route would be through a good agricultural district and the total length of the line from Muir of Ord to Cromarty would be 26 miles. Proposed stations were near the farm at Mains of Raddery, Braelangwell and Davidston. A branch was also proposed to the harbour at Cromarty. On 29th March Cromarty Town Council met to consider a letter from Innes & Mackay, the Inverness solicitors for the Great North, seeking support for their current proposed line, which of course did not come near the town. The matter was deferred awaiting confirmation of the Highland's proposals. These came in a letter dated 3rd April confirming that the extension to Cromarty could be built without difficulty and that if their proposed line to Fortrose was passed by Parliament the directors would favourably consider the early extension of the line to Cromarty, and if that was sanctioned by Parliament they would construct it. It was interesting that the letter suggested that the current proposal was for a line to Fortrose, when permission was being sought for a line through to Chanonry Point. The Town Council thus decided that they would not favour the Great North, the Highland being more attractive. The Great North responded by indicating that they were considering various options for routes to extend their line beyond Fortrose to include Cromarty and the northern side of the Black Isle, it being impossible to include these extensions in the present Bill. They intended to obtain the benefit of local opinion before determining the final route, but if their present Bill was passed the extension to Cromarty might be sought in the following Parliamentary session. A public meeting was held on 15th April which recommended that the Council petition in favour of both companies. The following day, despite a resolution that they favour the Great North, the decision was that it was unnecessary at present to petition in favour of either company.

Dingwall had also become involved. Despite protests at the short notice given, the Town Council met on Friday 4th April to receive the solicitors representing the two railway companies, Mr Innes for the Great North and Mr Duncan representing the Highland. Once again the Highland's past attitude of ignoring requests for improvements to their services was held against them, and the proposal was that the Town Council petition in favour of the Great North, although neither line came near Dingwall. There was a discussion on the further development of the Great North scheme which could result in a bridge over the end of the Cromarty Firth at Alcaig to complete a circle of the Black Isle by bringing the railway into Dingwall. The firth narrowed at this point and there were long wooden piers on both sides for the long-established ferry. Mr Duncan had little to say other than to suggest that the Highland were old friends of the burgh and ask that the matter be deferred until the company was in a position to state its case. The following Monday a lively meeting of local merchants and traders was held in the Dingwall Court Room. Lengthy discussion revolved round the possible loss of trade in Dingwall if the Highland scheme for a line, possibly eventually starting in Cromarty, took the agricultural produce and livestock from the Black Isle through Muir of Ord to Inverness rather than to the markets in Dingwall. The Great North, with their suggestion of completing a circle to bring the line into Dingwall, was much preferred, although doubt was cast over the bridge required at Alcaig. Instead of a bridge, a steam ferry had been suggested for the crossing. Mr Duncan was asked for the Highland's opinion on such a ferry. He considered that a steam ferry would be very expensive and that the Highland Railway could not attempt the impossible. It was thought that the Great North were also proposing to employ what they called a gathering steamer to ply between Portmahomack, Balintore and Cromarty to feed into their rail services at the new Campbelltown terminus, but of course there was no mention of this in the Bill presently before Parliament. The meeting eventually decided unanimously in favour of the Great North, as there was the possibility of Dingwall eventually benefitting from the Black Isle line, but the motion included the statement that no scheme for a Black Isle railway would be satisfactory which did not provide for a railway between Cromarty and Dingwall by way of a bridge over the Alcaig Ferry with its terminus at Dingwall.

The Town Council met again on 10th April. The Highland had by this time obtained advice from London to the effect that proposed discussion before the Town Council of Railways Bills now before Parliament might be resented by the Committee of the House of Commons as an attempt to forestall their enquiry and decision and might infringe any privilege of Parliament. They had been told not to attend the Council meeting. Mr Duncan, the Highland solicitor, was present but stated that he was there only in his capacity as a private individual and therefore was entitled to be there. After a stormy meeting the decision was taken, by one vote, to support neither scheme. The alternative had been support for the Great North. Despite several meetings and heated debates neither company had any support in the form of petitions from either Cromarty or Dingwall.

CHAPTER 3

THE FIGHT FOR THE BLACK ISLE

At the shareholders' meeting of the Highland Railway held on 29th October 1889, the chairman stated that they proposed constructing the railway to the Black Isle "and of course, if our opponents do not withdraw, it will be for us to consider whether the company should not make a fight for the possession of the Black Isle". That fight was to come to a conclusion within Committee Room 6 of the House of Commons where the Select Committee on Railway Bills met on 23rd April 1890. The Committee comprised four members under the chairmanship of Sir Richard Paget. The first bill under consideration was that of the Great North of Scotland Railway, which was principally for its line from Elgin to Inverness, but included their Black Isle branch. On the walls of the room, overlooking the River Thames, hung two immense maps, one showing the whole Scottish railway system, while the other covered the area between Elgin and Muir of Ord showing the proposed new Great North lines. Both companies brought huge boxes and portmanteaux crammed with documents. Representing the Great North were the chairman, William Ferguson of Kinmundy, accompanied by William Moffatt, secretary and general manager. Both had held their positions since 1879 and were experienced in the problems which had arisen in the last decade with the Highland. In addition various other officials were present as well as counsel, who opened the case for the Great North. The history of the two companies and the railway between Aberdeen and Inverness was explained to the Select Committee: *The Great North desired to be placed in a position to compete on better terms with the Highland, who carried on the competition in a way not equalled by any other company in the United Kingdom.* Referring to the Black Isle, counsel said that the company had been approached by a number of leading people there and asked to construct the line. This seems to be going somewhat beyond what had actually happened, as it was the Company itself which had been assiduous in soliciting local support. Several letters were read regarding the proposed amalgamation of the companies, but that was not a matter for the committee. Several witnesses from the Black Isle, including Mr Fletcher, were present, the evidence being conducted from one end of the line to the other.

There were over a score of objections to the Elgin to Inverness line, but almost all the Black Isle evidence was in favour of the Great North and gave a fascinating insight into life there before the coming of the railway, demonstrating its insular position and the great necessity for improvements in transport links. Colin Mackenzie Cameron, Factor of Kilcoy Estate, and the son of James Cameron who in 1872 had collected much information on potential traffic for a railway in the Black Isle, supplied evidence on the difficulties and expense which the farmers faced. Barley was occasionally sold to Thornbush Brewery in Inverness. This had to be carted the seven mile distance to the Kessock Ferry, the brewery being just half a mile from the southern ferry jetty. The barley was nearly always damaged due to exposure to the sea and weather on the ferry crossing. A large quantity of barley was grown on the Black Isle, the quality being as good as any grown anywhere in Scotland. The brewers had stated that were it not for the risks attending the ferry crossing they would take all the barley they required from the Black Isle. Better prices and higher sales would be achieved if the Great North line was built. Similar advantages would accrue in the purchase of feeding stuffs from Aberdeen. Manure at present was purchased from Mr Cran at Bunchrew. It was shipped across the Beauly Firth and landed at Munlochy Bay, where the boat was beached and could be unloaded only at low tide. The Black Isle was greatly valued as a safe wintering district for hill sheep, and the railway would be well used in their transport from and back to various parts of the Highlands. The sheep came principally from the west. The Great North being an east coast company, this point was not mentioned!

Mr Cameron indicated the difficulties he had in seeking tenants for the mansion houses at Kilcoy and Drynie when enquirers discovered that the houses could only be reached by crossing the Kessock Ferry. The rents of many properties were much below those achieved in other districts. A similar problem arose in letting farms, rents paid being on a much lower scale than for similar land more favourably situated as to transport links. There were effectively only three routes by which stock, grain and goods could be transported to or from the Kilcoy area, namely by road and ferry to or from Inverness, by road to Muir of Ord station, or by sailing vessels which at certain states of the tide could be beached in Munlochy Bay. Timber felled in the area was either carted to Muir of Ord or taken by sailing ship from Munlochy Bay.

He considered that the Highland scheme was 'crude and incomplete', brought forward only with a view to trying to prevent the Great North from achieving its line. He noted that the Highland had no proposals for the ferry at Fort George, other than to build lines to both terminals. He considered that the thinking behind this was to leave the Fort George ferry so unattractive that passengers and goods traffic bound for Inverness and the south and east would prefer to travel the much longer distance via Muir of Ord.

John Smith had been a merchant in Fortrose for 33 years and gave evidence on the problems faced in that district. He explained the difficulties which could arise in using the existing ferryboat at Fort George detailed in the previous chapter and considered that the current difficulties with road vehicles at Fort George would remain if the Highland station at Fort George was sited at the intended distance from the usual landing place on the beach at the west side of the fort. The goods for sale in his shop came from Thornbush, about a mile from Inverness station, to Fortrose by steamer. The cost of shipping forward from Inverness was approximately half of the cost of transport from Glasgow or Edinburgh to Inverness. Prior to the steamer being put on from Inverness by the Black Isle Steam Shipping Company in 1882 all his goods had to be brought to Muir of Ord and thence by cart to Fortrose. Goods were also brought in from Leith and Aberdeen by the steamer *Earnholm* to Inverness. This ship came north once per week, usually arriving in Inverness on a Wednesday night, but the goods did not reach Fortrose until Saturday; deliveries from London could take up to ten days. Other goods came from Liverpool and Glasgow, arriving in Inverness via the Caledonian Canal and thence being carted from Muirtown at the head of the canal to the Thornbush pier to be brought by steamer to Fortrose. As many suppliers' terms were 'carriage paid to nearest railway station' the saving to Mr Smith would be around six shillings per ton once Fortrose had its own station.

The railway would greatly increase the number of tourists and visitors, although it was admitted that in 1889 every house in the district available for visitors was occupied. On most days between June and September the *Rosehaugh* made one return trip daily between Inverness and Fortrose, although this was increased on certain days. During the winter months the steamer ran only two or three days each week. In May 1893 for example it departed Fortrose every Tuesday and Friday at 9.30 am, returning from Inverness at 4.30 pm on Tuesdays and 4 pm on Fridays. In July of that year there were two crossings daily on Mondays and Thursdays, three on Saturdays, and one on the other three days. There were no Sunday sailings. House building in the area was costly as stones for the buildings in Fortrose were taken in by sea. Many of the houses in the town were built of stone from the Mulbine quarry, between Covesea and Hopeman on the Moray coast, transport costing 4/8d per ton. Suddie and Kilcoy quarries would be close to the railway, providing easier and cheaper transport for future building work.

Further evidence on the benefits likely to accrue to the district were given by John Henderson, Fortrose Town Clerk, who was also the factor and commissioner for Rosehaugh Estate, managing partner of the firm Alexander Henderson, coal lime and agricultural contractor, and general merchant in both Fortrose and Avoch. He had been in trade in the area for 22 years, and was also a ship owner and general manager and secretary of the Black Isle Steam Shipping Company. As such he was likely to lose trade through the competition from the railway, but nonetheless he was strongly in favour of the Great North. He stressed the want of a more direct and easy communication with the rest of the country, cut off as the Black Isle was by its insular position and the inconvenience of having to cross the Firth by what he described as 'troublesome open ferries'. One of the area's principal products was potatoes. They were shipped to Newcastle, Sunderland, Portsmouth, London and other places. If sent by rail they would reach their destination much more quickly and in far better condition than going by sea, being subjected to damage on board ship and in subsequent transhipment into railway trucks. Potatoes sent by rail were worth at least 10/- per ton more than when sent by sea. They would also catch markets which were missed due to the long sea journeys. At the time he gave his evidence, Mr Henderson was able to indicate that there was a ship which had been loaded for ten days but had been unable to leave Cromarty on account of the head winds, the result of which was great inconvenience and likely financial loss. Potatoes sent by rail would not have to be bagged, saving a further 5/- or 6/- per ton.

The Great North, through their steamer connection, would open up grain markets in Elgin, Huntly and Aberdeen as well as the numerous distilleries in Banffshire and Morayshire. At the present time the farmers within a five mile radius of Fortrose sent the bulk of their grain by sea from Fortrose to Inverness and beyond. Animals were sold at the auctions in Inverness or to cattle dealers in Keith or Inverurie. Some farmers sent their beasts by the Kessock Ferry while others used the Fort George crossing, the latter requiring a four mile walk to the Fort George station on the Inverness to Nairn line. Fat sheep and pigs were similarly despatched from the Black Isle, while 15,000 pairs of hares and rabbits were exported from Fortrose, mainly to Sheffield. 1,000 pheasants and 2,000 brace of partridges were sent by steamer to Inverness. During 1889 nine thousand sheep had travelled in the opposite direction for wintering east of Munlochy. The total quantity of goods shipped and unshipped in sailing vessels during 1889 had been 7,354 tons at Fortrose and 2,395 at Avoch, in addition to the 1,710 tons dealt with at Fortrose on the *Rosehaugh*.

Another commodity which would greatly benefit from rail transport was lime. Mr Henderson explained that it did not 'stand much knocking about' and had always deteriorated by being first carried in railway trucks and then forwarded by ship. Most came from England, but some came from Keith although it was 5/- per ton dearer than the English product, and was subject to the same problems of transport, being taken by rail to Lossiemouth or Burghead and thence by sea to Fortrose. Coal for consumption on the Black Isle was deposited from ships on various beaches, for example Munlochy, Corgrain, Kessock Pier, Findon and Cullicudden. Local people were then put to much inconvenience and expense in the onward carting of the coal. The Great North proposals were much more attractive than those of the Highland. Mr Henderson was sure that passengers and goods coming from the south and intended for the Black Isle and places north of Muir of Ord would much prefer to use the Great North's steamer from Campbelltown to Fortrose than go through Inverness. He stressed the lack of provision being made in the Highland scheme for the passage of passengers or goods across the Firth at Fort George. The Highland appeared intent on landing passengers, livestock and goods in the neighbourhood of the beach and allowing them to find their own way across as best they could. Such a scheme was described by Mr Henderson as 'unfinished and utterly unworkable'.

Murdo Macrae, mason at Kilcoy, gave evidence on the quarries near to the proposed line. There were freestone quarries at Tarradale and Kilcoy, the latter being of a better quality, easier to quarry and dress. It was possible to produce upwards of 30,000 tons per week. The proposed Great North station at Tore would suit the Kilcoy quarry admirably, being within half a mile of the workings. At the time it lay 7 miles from the nearest railway at Muir of Ord. The cost of carriage was 9d per ton per mile, which was so great that it prevented the sale of stone outwith the immediate district. Suddie quarry was also freestone, but much softer than the others. It was however good stone and useful for some purposes although possibly it would not last as long as the others. Redcastle quarry was deeper than the others, but it would be over two miles from any station on the new line. Mr Macrae maintained that no quarry east of Covesea could compete with Black Isle quarries.

James Douglas Fletcher, proprietor of Rosehaugh Estate, was firmly in favour of the Great North proposals as being a complete scheme. He too doubted the sincerity of the Highland who had had ample opportunity and encouragement in the past quarter century to build a line through the Black Isle had they wished. He brought out the potential benefits to Avoch, the nearest village to Rosehaugh and situated on his land. Hitherto it had languished by reason of its fishermen having no means whereby they could get their fish to the markets of the south in a fresh condition. The Great North scheme would suit them best as by its means they could put their fish on the rails at Campbelltown and so on to a main line leading to the various southern markets where sales could be effected. He had explained that with the imminent opening of the Highland Railway's direct line from Aviemore to Inverness, the existing line east from Inverness would be relegated to branch line status, 'and become subject to all the disadvantages to which branch lines are usually subjected'. The Great North pier at Campbelltown would be on their main line. Thus he did not envisage the Avoch fishermen using the Black Isle railway, but he did join with others in expressing the advantages likely to accrue to farmers, timber merchants and quarrymen.

Support for the Great North was not total. Two landowners objected to their proposed route. The line was intended to pass through the Wester Suddie estate owned by George McLean of Drynie for a distance of 1 mile and 1 chain. It would sever in a most injurious manner very valuable arable land without any compensating advantage. The route of the Highland's line would not injure his property in any way and was quite acceptable. Like Rev John Gibson of Avoch, whose objection to the Great North was also due to the route the line was to take, Mr McLean pointed out that there were doubts as to the company's ability to raise the funds to build all its intended lines, having paid an average dividend of 15/- per cent on its ordinary stock over the last twenty years. It seems more than likely, as the exact terminology was used by both, that the information was supplied to both objectors by the Highland!

Colonel Roderick G Mackenzie of Flowerburn was another petitioner against the Great North. He was owner of the estate of Flowerburn in Fortrose which was intended to be intersected in an extremely injurious manner by the line. Land very suitable for building and feuing purposes was to be taken and 'injured to a high degree' by the construction. Colonel Mackenzie was also the owner of the ancient right of ferry between Fort George Point and Chanonry Point. This ferry, he maintained, was the natural and only regular means of communication over the Moray Firth east of Kessock Ferry and its preservation as a ferry in active and constant use was not only of material importance to him as the owner of the ferry, but was of great consequence to the public. The Great North's Bill proposed an infringement of his rights by running a steam ferry between Campbelltown and Fortrose without making any compensation whatever to him. The Highland's proposed lines, on both sides of the firth, would afford a much better means of communication between the Black Isle and the south and the east than the Great North proposals, the distance between the ferry piers at Fort George and Chanonry Point being only one third of the distance between Campbelltown and Fortrose. In addition, the Highland line would serve the growing village of Rosemarkie at that time much favoured as a health resort. Again probably prompted by the Highland, the Colonel repeated the opinion voiced by Rev Gibson that the railway was badly designed in its engineering details.

A week was spent by the Committee hearing the evidence for and against the Great North's proposed lines, those heard including over twenty objectors to the line between Elgin and Inverness. On 29th April, after hearing three Members of Parliament, Dr Hunter and Mr Esslemont of Aberdeen North and East, and Mr Leng of Dundee, who were in favour, the room was cleared for the members of the committee to consider what they had heard. On the readmission of the public, the chairman announced that so much of the preamble as related to the proposed line between Elgin and Inverness had not been proved. It was left to the promoters whether they wished to proceed with the lines in the Black Isle and from Elgin to Hopeman and Burghead. The Great North immediately abandoned their idea of a line in the Black Isle, but proceeded to set forth their case for the latter, although it too was rejected.

In reporting the result to the Great North directors, the chairman explained the necessity to withdraw the Black Isle line and the ferry as they would have been so isolated. He stated that the select Committee from the first stopped their evidence, declined to hear anything of the difficulties with the Highland Railway Company and gave their decision without hearing the other side at all. The Great North's defeat was felt north of the Black Isle. A letter was sent to them from Wick Town Council, thanking them for their efforts to extend railways in the north of Scotland and hoping that in the public interest further efforts might be made notwithstanding the unfortunate result for the general public in the north of Scotland of the defeat of the bill before Parliament by the Great North of Scotland Railway Company. There was obviously substantial support for a competitor to come into the Highland Railway's area, and more than a hint of bias in the Select Committee.

This decision caused great disappointment in the Black Isle, not the least to Mr Fletcher of Rosehaugh, whose favouring of the Great North now turned into antagonism towards the Highland. He was not present at the Committee hearing, but immediately on the announcement of the failure of the Great North scheme a telegram was despatched from the telegraph office in Parliament by the Great North Parliamentary Agent to the company's Inverness solicitor, Charles Innes of Innes & Mackay: *Get hold of Mr Fletcher of Rosehaugh. Arrange to have him here tomorrow at ten and be with him.* The following morning Mr Fletcher telegraphed from Avoch telegraph office to Innes, then staying at the Carlton Club in London: *Object to Highland Scheme for me*. In answer to a request for his grounds for objection, that evening Fletcher telegraphed again: *You can say my opposition is spontaneous and I would have given evidence against Highland personally if I had known it would be necessary*. To this the immediate response of Innes was that he would say on Fletcher's behalf that he distinctly objected for reasons in his proof to the Highland Scheme, but it was essential that he have a reply by ten tomorrow for it to be of any use.

On 1st May the Select Committee reconvened to consider the Highland Bills, which comprised the line through the Black Isle from Muir of Ord to Chanonry Point, the branch from the existing line east of Inverness at Fort George station to the Fort itself and the extension of their existing branch to Burghead a further two miles to Hopeman. There was no opposition to the lines to Fort George and Hopeman, and only two objections to the Black Isle line. The Burgh of Fortrose, having been in favour of the Great North, had formally intimated an objection to the Highland, but, being neither present nor represented at the hearing, their opposition was not considered. The only remaining objector was Mr Fletcher who was not present, but was represented by Mr Cripps QC. Mr Claude Baggallay QC, presenting the case for the Highland, stated that Mr Fletcher, in his evidence in favour of the Great North, had agreed that it was a line that should be built, and that he, Fletcher, preferred the Great North Scheme. Mr Baggallay pointed out that the Great North line had been laid out to go through Mr Fletcher's estate and across his access road, but that the Highland line would not pass through his estate and would pass a distance of five furlongs from his house. All Mr Fletcher was doing was expressing a preference between the two schemes, not making a valid objection. He also indicated that the line had been laid out in such a way that it could in the future, if thought desirable, be extended towards the north to Cromarty.

Andrew Dougall, secretary and general manager of the Highland Railway, was then examined. After stressing the high quality of service provided by the company, 'running the quickest single line service in Britain', he indicated that they had thought that there should have been a line in the Black Isle as long ago as 1872, but the project fell through, despite giving a verbal offer to the late Mr Fletcher of funding for the line amounting to £10,000. Murdoch Paterson CE, chief engineer of the Highland, stated that he had designed the line in such a way as to do as little damage to Mr Fletcher's property as possible, having obtained the late Mr Fletcher's consent to his proposals. Alexander Ross, Provost of Inverness, confirmed that he was an architect in Inverness and that he had built Mr Fletcher's house and entrance gate. In his opinion the line would not interfere with the view from his grounds.

Sir Richard Paget, the Select Committee chairman, observed that no powers were sought for a ferry between Chanonry and Fort George, and asked whether the Highland Company, if they got their bill, would be willing to improve the existing ferry so that cattle and other heavy traffic arriving in the district and going to the east might be sent by the ferry instead of going round by Muir of Ord. It was accepted that the present ferry was very small, but piers could easily be constructed at either side and a new ferry might be put on if it was desired. The Committee considered that the ferry should be properly developed. Mr Pember QC, for the Highland, stated: *I think I can give an undertaking that the Highland Company would do all they could to foster that route by Fort George*. The chairman asked if that was a pledge. *It is one of those pledges which counsel give and which can be brought up against the railway company on a future occasion if it is not kept. I can give a pledge that the Highland Company will do their best to make that right available for the public on proper terms. I give it in the strongest possible way and it will be brought up against the Highland if they do not fulfil it. The pledge has been made in all seriousness, deliberately and candidly*. It was pointed out that Mr Fletcher appeared to be opposing the Highland Railway scheme which was practically the same as the Great North scheme of which he had given evidence in support. All that could be said in defence of his objection was that knowing the extreme importance of the development of railway accommodation in the Black Isle he did not want the Highland line to be passed because it did not adequately meet all the requirements of the Black Isle and if it was passed no other line could ever be brought forward. Suddenly, without reverting to counsel for the Highland, the chairman brought matters to an abrupt conclusion by saying: *This is a matter that the committee are unanimous upon. The preamble of the Bill is proved.*

Mr Fletcher was immediately telegraphed to the effect that 'after a stiff fight' the Highland Bill had been passed and that the Highland counsel, on being pressed by the chairman, had given a pledge that improvements would be made to the ferry. His response was that he would oppose the Bill if a clause for the ferry was not inserted. Mr Innes was instructed to 'make a firm stand'. On 3rd May John Henderson, in his position as Estate factor for Rosehaugh, wrote to Mr Innes stating that Mr Fletcher asked if it was possible to arrange for an indignation meeting (a meeting held for the purpose of expressing and discussing grievances) against the rejection of the Great North lines and the granting of the Highland bill, and asking what steps should be taken to continue opposition to the Highland.

The Highland tried to calm matters. On 10th May their solicitors, Stewart Rule & Burns, wrote to Innes & Mackay who were acting for Mr Fletcher: *Now that the contest is over, the company hopes that Mr Fletcher will cordially accept the situation. He has manfully fought his battle and has lost it, unless he counts his loss, as we do, as gain. The Highland Company desires to re-establish amicable relations with Mr Fletcher and the Black Isle people and may count upon the directors doing everything in their power consistent with the situation.* 12th May brought a telegram from Mr Henderson to Mr Innes which demonstrated travel at the time: *I go to Inverness by steamer tomorrow. Will call.*

There was still a possibility of stopping the Highland. The bill was read for the first time in the House of Lords on 16th May, which, unless the House adjourned earlier for the Whitsuntide recess, would result in the time for petitioning against it expiring on the 23rd. Dyson & Co, parliamentary agents, advised Innes & Mackay that it would be practically impossible to introduce into the Bill at the present stage any provisions binding the Highland Company to establish or work a ferry or piers even if the company desired to facilitate such an alteration. There was a petition going forward from allotment holders in Campbelltown whose ground would be interfered with. Dyson & Co sent a draft of a form of petition to Innes & Mackay for completion. At this time Charles Innes was in what to this day remains one of the most remote places in the country, Knoydart, but was kept informed of what was happening by his partner. The nearest telegraph office to which the telegram could be sent was Isleornsay in Skye!

Fletcher's opposition ended. On 19th May Henderson wrote to Innes & Mackay: *As there does not appear to be any desire amongst the people down here to offer any opposition to the Highland scheme and a considerable number flatter themselves with the idea that all will come right if they only get a railway, Mr Fletcher is not inclined to enter upon the contest single handed and at the same time very possibly against the wishes of many of the inhabitants of the district.* Fortrose Town Council, while expressing their sorrow that the Great North had been defeated, decided that if Mr Fletcher was not proceeding further neither would they.

The Highland Railway (New Lines) Bill was read a third time and was passed in the House of Lords on 24th June 1890. The way was at last clear for a railway to be built in the Black Isle.

WHYTE, PHOTO-ARTIST,   INVERNESS

THE BLACK ISLE RAILWAY.

LAYING OF KEYSTONE MUNLOCHY BURN BRIDGE.

24th JUNE 1892.

The laying of the keystone for the Munlochy Burn bridge on 24th June 1892. The culvert through the embankment still exists but the stonework in this photograph is now totally obscured by a curtain of ivy.   *(White, Inverness/Highland Railway Society colln)*

CHAPTER 4

CONSTRUCTION AND OPENING

There had, of course, been great doubt in the Black Isle as to whether, if successful in their fight with the Great North for the area, the Highland would ever build the line. It was admitted that there was no great population to be served, but the area was one of rich farmland and was increasingly attracting summer visitors. In one of his letters to Charles Innes, the Inverness solicitor acting for the Great North, the Provost of Fortrose had added: *I hope you are coming down this way this season to the sea side. The Grahams at Cromarty want to let their house. If you can send a tenant their way they will be much obliged.*

On 9th October 1890 the Highland Railway issued the 'Specification for the Construction of the Black Isle Railway extending from Muir of Ord station to the town of Fortrose'. There was no mention of Rosemarkie or Chanonry Point. Nor was there any movement to build the line to the Fort from the existing Fort George station on the Inverness – Elgin line. It was 1898 before this branch was built, and then only as far as the village of Campbelltown. In addition to the single line to Fortrose the specification required the construction of about 2 miles 275 yards of sidings and connections and 28 sets of switches and crossings with stations at Kilcoy, Tore, Munlochy, Avoch and Fortrose. Completion was anticipated by 1st July 1892. On 28th October the offer of John Ross & Son of Fearn to construct the line for the sum of £54,347.13.11d plus £500 for six months' maintenance was accepted. Work began on 19th November. Ross was one of the most successful contractors in the north of Scotland, following in his father's footsteps and with his own eldest son coming behind him. He had started as a road contractor, keeping in excellent repair many of the roads in Easter Ross, and already had experience of constructing the railway from Keith to Portessie and part of the Sutherland & Caithness Railway. At the time he was involved in the construction of the first portion of the new direct line north from Aviemore as far as Carr Bridge, from where he had put in his tender.

The price excluded, of course, the land and also the rails, chairs, fishplates, fishbolts, sleepers and wooden buffer beams which would be delivered by the Highland Railway to the contractor at Muir of Ord. The construction of the station buildings and houses for agents and crossing keepers was the subject of separate contracts, but John Ross was required to construct all necessary platforms and to supply the 48,000 teak wood keys and 56 tons of wrought iron spikes needed for the track. The price of laying 23,760 yards of rail was £1,188, while the provision and laying of 47,520 cubic yards of ballast cost £4,752. The Highland also supplied the iron straining pillars, the wooden posts and the wire for fencing the line. Ross was to be paid at the rate of 6d per yard for unloading these items

John Ross, Contractor

at Muir of Ord, conveying them to the line and having the fences erected by competent fencers. A total of 48,000 yards of fencing was required, giving a total price of £1,200. Some of the larger quantities involved in the construction were 395,850 cubic yards of cutting through earth and clay, 45,640 cubic yards of cutting through rock, 315,370 cubic yards of embankment and 250,000 square yards of soiling slopes of cuttings and embankments including the sowing of grass seeds. The total cost of the line was estimated at around £100,000.

There were no major engineering works such as viaducts or tunnels, and the bridges were almost all in respect of crossings of public or occupation roads, with numerous cattle creeps and culverts taking several burns under the line, usually where the line was on an embankment. The largest bridge was the only steel girder one, namely that crossing the public road at Linnie. It had originally been intended that the bridge taking the estate road at Avoch over the line be a girder bridge, but it was constructed, like all others on the line except Linnie, in stone and brick. The original plans included two bridges over the line between Avoch and Fortrose which were not built. The first was in Avoch itself carrying the public road adjacent to the Established Church and the second for an occupation road which rose steeply from the Avoch – Fortrose road to the terrace above Craig Wood. The first was not required as the former estate road became a public road, Mackenzie Place, and the second was not built as the occupation road was closed. The platform at Fortrose, at 597 ft, was somewhat shorter than the original intended length of 778 ft, but the intermediate stations were around 450 ft, only 35 ft less than indicated in the tender documents.

Within a year, in deference to the estates through which the line was to pass, the names of the first two stations were changed to Redcastle and Allangrange. Colonel Burton Mackenzie, who had recently restored Kilcoy Castle which was close to the proposed site of the station, attempted to have the name of Redcastle changed to Kilcoy in a letter to the Highland directors in October 1891, but to no avail. Despite the relative ease with which the line could be constructed, it took over four years to build. Work commenced without ceremony on Monday 24th November 1890 and in May the following year it was still anticipated that the line would open at the end of June 1892. Following resumption of work after the New Year break in 1891 there were 140 men at work, principally involved in the digging of cuttings between Muir of Ord and Kilcoy. There was no major influx of navvies in the district recorded in the 1891 census. Most of the labourers were resident locally. However there were quite a number of Gaelic speakers who had come from the west involved in the building of the line. John Cameron was regarded as a Gaelic scholar in the district and was often called upon to read and write letters for those Gaelic speakers.

The work was not without danger. On 20th May 1891 the gaffer of one of the gangs, a tall middle aged man by the name of Chisholm, was standing below a bank of gravel at Munlochy above which his men were working. The bank suddenly gave way and Chisholm was buried alive under the soil. He was extricated without delay and medical help was quickly summoned, but, despite rallying in the next two days, he died of his injuries on the 23rd in the house at which he was lodging locally. During 1891 work continued in the Munlochy area. By October a number of men were employed in piling the foundation for the bridge to be erected behind the southern portion of the village where a large embankment was to be constructed. The keystone for the culvert taking the burn through this embankment was laid, in the presence of several of the villagers, on 24th June 1892.

Following the placing of an advertisement for tenders which appeared in the 1891 Christmas Day issue of the *Inverness Courier*, on 11th February 1892 offers were considered

The agent's house at Avoch in 1909, situated on the main road and still looking remarkably similar today. James Morrison, station master, had transferred from Redcastle in December 1908 and is seen with his sons Iain (with the dog) and Graham.   *(SRPS/Iain Morrison collection)*

for the construction of the station buildings. Andrew Mackintosh & Sons of Redcastle were successful with their prices of £449.13.2d each for Redcastle and Munlochy, £453.7.2d for Avoch and £454.2.6d for Allangrange. Fortrose, being a larger station at the terminus, was more expensive at £602.4.7d. W & R Maclean of Dingwall were awarded the contract for the agent's house at Redcastle (£354.8.7d) and porters' houses there (£328.13.5d) as well as at Allangrange where the agent's house was £363.13.8d and the porter's houses £333. 3.0d. Alexander Barclay of Keith was to build the agent's house at Avoch for £362.18.11d and the surfacemen's houses at Corrachie for £316.16.2d.

By the end of February 1892 the track was laid from Muir of Ord to the neighbourhood of Redcastle, and it was anticipated that the contractor's engine would soon reach Allangrange. There was heavy work still required between Munlochy and Avoch, where a great deal of local interest had been raised by the 'new steam digger or navvy crane' in use. It weighed 38 tons and had caused some trouble before being brought into action, but when in full operation it required seven men to produce the output of fifty navvies. It was principally involved in digging out the cuttings near Avoch and depositing the spoil in the valley in front of Avoch House forming the embankments on either side of the bridge over the burn.

The following winter was not kind to railway builders in the Highlands. In addition to the Black Isle line, John Ross was working on the first section of the new line north from Aviemore as far as Carr Bridge, which opened on 8th July 1892. Long spells of intense frost interrupted stone building work and rendered work by squads of navvies well nigh impossible. It began to seem unlikely that the opening date of 1st July 1892 as specified in the contract would be met.

All was not well in Avoch, however. The villagers were concerned at the proposed location of the station which would be about a mile from the centre of the village. They therefore considered that they would not derive any convenience or benefit from the new railway owing to this very inconvenient and disadvantageous location. On 14th September 1891 a deputation met Andrew Dougall, general manager, and four separate petitions were sent to the directors of the Highland Railway, but no satisfactory responses were received. The difficulty would appear to have been that if the station had been located to the east of the crossing of the burn, nearer the centre of the village, it would have been on a 1 in 60 gradient, which would not have been permitted by the Board of Trade. It is unlikely that this was understood by the villagers, who, possibly not unreasonably, considered that by erecting the station a mile distant from the busiest part of the village, the Highland Railway was thereby diminishing the traffic which would naturally flow to its line and were also crippling the trade of Avoch. The solution found was to attach to the bridge over the burn a cantilevered walkway for a footpath alongside the south side of the line to provide a link to the station from the houses at the area of the village near the Established Church. The path commenced with an ornamental wooden stairway leading down from Mackenzie Place.

Despite this problem, as soon as it was known that the railway was to be built to Avoch, building improvements were commenced. Among these were the buildings of the Caledonian Bank and the Post Office. For many years commercial travellers and others had felt the lack of a hotel in the village. This was remedied in June 1892 with the opening by Mr James Finlayson of a handsome and commodious new building at the then west end of the village, being fitted out with all modern improvements as a hotel, and having a dining room capable of accommodating around forty diners. It was designed by Mr Mackintosh, architect of Inverness. Despite its distance from the line it was named the Station Hotel.

By November 1892 work was concentrated on the section between Munlochy and Fortrose. The station at Munlochy, described as being a convenient and suitable structure with comfortable waiting rooms for passengers, had been erected and work had started on the construction of the station at Avoch. The local people continued to be most impressed by the work done by the steam navvy but much remained to be done between Munlochy and Avoch. All stations had only one platform, there being no crossing loops on the line. The building at Fortrose was larger than the intermediate stations. It had separate general and ladies' waiting rooms, booking office and station master's office.

The workmen were on the whole well behaved. The Kirk Session of the Free Church at Avoch in considering the religion and morals, Sabbath observance and Sabbath Schools during 1893 were 'thankful to find that the state of morals and Sabbath observance among the people of the congregation and in the parish had been satisfactory, especially considering the influx of strangers to the district during the construction of the Black Isle Railway'.

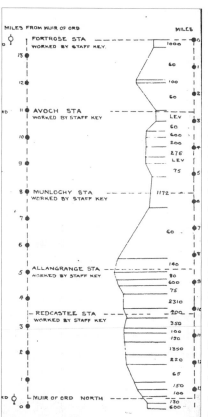

The gradient diagram of the branch with the junction at Muir of Ord at the bottom.

There were the occasional miscreants among the navvies. Two appeared at Dingwall Sheriff Court on 14th June 1892. Murdo Morrison was fined 2/6 for breach of the peace while Andrew Munro was fined 15/- for breach of the peace and assault. On 13th May the following year Simon Mackenzie was fined 7/6 for breach of the peace.

Once again, Cromarty Town Council attempted to have the line extended to their town. The directors of the Highland Railway asked for a statement of the probable traffic and an indication of how much capital the Council would provide towards the construction. Nothing further was heard from them at this time.

The final fortnight of March 1893 was particularly fine and by this time the cutting behind Munlochy had been completed and the rails laid from Muir of Ord as far as East Gateside farm, about a mile east of Munlochy. Near the site of Fortrose station a number of old coins were found by workmen, but nearly all were coppers. Murdoch Paterson, the Highland Railway engineer, took up residence at Bon-Accord Villa in Fortrose from 12th April, and the opening was anticipated in the autumn.

During the summer of 1893 the station agents for the new line were appointed. Simon Mackenzie, agent at Halkirk, was to move to Fortrose. Mr Sim from the goods department at Inverness was appointed to Avoch, while John Taylor, currently agent at Achanalt, was to go to Munlochy. John Macrae, spare pointsman at Inverness, was to have Allangrange, and John Archibald, booking clerk at Dingwall, filled the new post at Redcastle. He had been very popular during his four years at Dingwall, being described at the presentation of a purse of sovereigns to him on his departure as "one of the nicest young men who was ever sent out of Dingwall". In addition to this gift from the passengers, the railway staff presented him with a Gladstone bag, as well as a beautiful pipe and tobacco pouch.

On Wednesday 1st November 1893 the track was completed between Muir of Ord and Fortrose, many unforeseen difficulties having arisen such as the heavy rock cuttings and embankments required in the Craig Wood between Avoch and Fortrose. A sad accident took place on this stretch on 10th November when an 18 year old lad, John Gillies from Port of Ness in the Isle of Lewis, was fatally injured when he overbalanced and fell from a wagon immediately behind the engine. Eventually all was ready and on 20th January 1894 Murdoch Paterson wrote to Major Marindin, the Board of Trade inspector:-

After a protracted struggle with very changeable weather and other adverse circumstances we have at last succeeded in bringing the works of this line to a close. I have been at Fortrose for the last 8 days and return there this afternoon. We have very mild weather and hope it will continue until you have done with your inspection. I sincerely regret the awkward season of the year in which we have asked you to come north.

The official inspection took place on Tuesday 30th January. Murdoch Paterson's hope that the very mild weather would continue was not fulfilled as the inspection was described as being made 'under the most uncomfortable atmospheric conditions'. Major Marindin was accompanied by Mr Dougall, the general manager, Mr Paterson and Mr Roberts the engineers, Mr Garrow, superintendent of the line, Mr Thomson, goods manager, Mr Jones, locomotive superintendent and other heads of department of the Highland Railway Company. Messrs Ross the contractors, and Murdoch Macdonald, resident engineer during the construction, were also present. Following the inspection, at the invitation of James Douglas Fletcher, the inspecting party was hospitably entertained at Rosehaugh House and returned to Inverness in the evening.

Major Marindin reported that the whole of the works were well and substantially

The only signal cabin on the branch was at Fortrose and there are few photographs which show it. This is an enlargement of one taken on 28th July 1913.

(J B Sherlock)

constructed. The length of the line was 13 miles 45 chains and there were no tunnels, viaducts or level crossings of public roads. He noted that in places the gradients were heavy, several being 1 in 60. The line was well ballasted with broken stone and fenced by post and wire fencing. There were only three major embankments, the longest being at a height of 52 feet with the two shorter ones reaching 70 and 59 feet. His report indicated that there were 13 overbridges, all with masonry abutments, and 17 bridges under the line. This disagrees with the Highland Railway's bridge register, which lists 12 overbridges and 23 underbridges, although it is likely that the Major ignored six creeps and culverts under eight feet span, several of which were placed deep below the line in embankments. He noted that each of the five stations had one platform 3ft in height and sufficient accommodation for passengers. The station at Muir of Ord, which had become a junction, had been improved and the platforms lengthened. The up platform was now an island platform and new station buildings were nearing completion. The signalling at Muir of Ord was in two cabins, the South one having 25 working levers and the North, which controlled the junction with the new branch, having 39 working levers. Each cabin had one spare lever.

The line was to be operated on the 'one engine in steam' principle using telegraphic block and train staff to which was attached an Annett's key for operating the ground frames at the intermediate stations. The Highland chairman, Eneas Mackintosh, and secretary Andrew Dougall, gave an undertaking to the effect that 'one engine only or two engines coupled together, carrying staff, would be on the branch line from Muir of Ord Junction to Fortrose at one and the same time'. At Fortrose there were sidings on both sides of the line, a loop, an engine turntable (there was also a turntable at Muir of Ord), and a signal cabin containing 17 working and 2 spare levers. The cabin was of the standard design used by the Highland Railway at the time, supplied by Dutton & Co. At the intermediate stations there was a one siding connection with facing points to down (Fortrose bound) trains, there being no signals other than a ground signal. The points were worked from a 3 lever ground frame locked by the train staff. Only minor corrective work was required, such as a buffer stop being erected at Fortrose at the end of one of the sidings. Subject to the minor works being undertaken within a week, and Muir of Ord station buildings completed within six weeks, the Major recommended that the opening of the Black Isle branch for passenger traffic could be sanctioned. On 17th February a report was sent to the Board of Trade confirming that all the requirements of the inspector

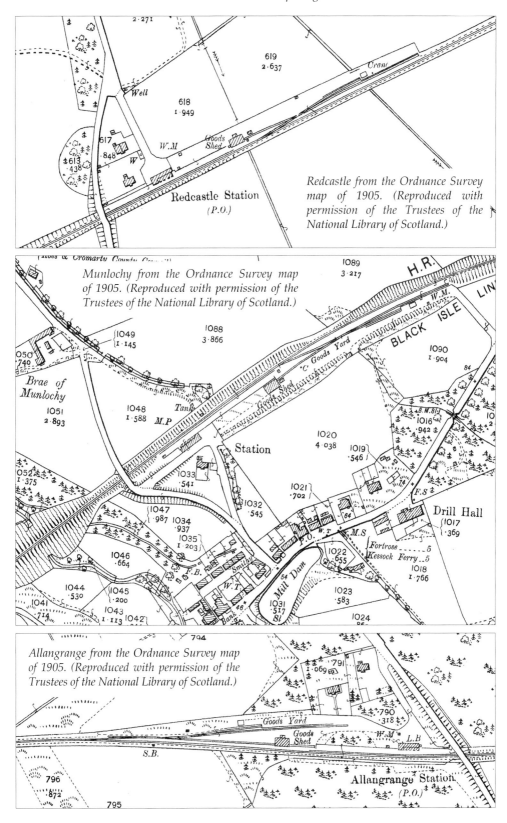

Redcastle from the Ordnance Survey map of 1905. (Reproduced with permission of the Trustees of the National Library of Scotland.)

Munlochy from the Ordnance Survey map of 1905. (Reproduced with permission of the Trustees of the National Library of Scotland.)

Allangrange from the Ordnance Survey map of 1905. (Reproduced with permission of the Trustees of the National Library of Scotland.)

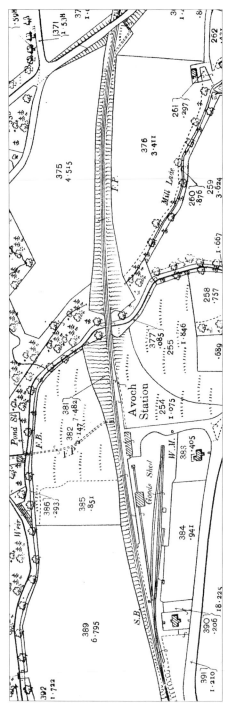

had been complied with, and this was followed on 23rd March by a report that the buildings at Muir of Ord had been completed and the waiting rooms and conveniences were being used by the public. Major Marindin returned to the area on 11th April and expressed his satisfaction with all that had been done.

From Muir of Ord the branch turned immediately east in a tight curve of 11 chains radius for 460 yards to cross the Muir of Tarradale. To the left for the next few miles could be seen the slopes of Millbuie Ridge covered with crofts and crofters' houses. Beyond Spital Wood fine scenery across the Beauly Firth came into view and just before arriving at Redcastle station Killearnan Free Church could be seen to the right, with Kilcoy Castle towering to the left. Restored to habitation in 1890 by Alexander Ross, architect of Inverness, for Colonel Burton Mackenzie, it was traditionally a hunting lodge of the Kings of Scotland and was an excellent example of sixteenth and seventeenth century architecture. About a mile to the south of the station was Redcastle itself, said, at the time of the opening of the railway, to be the oldest inhabited house in Scotland, dating back to 1179.

Leaving Redcastle the train passed the Free Church Manse on the left, crossing the private road to the manse on one of the two level crossings provided with a crossing keeper's cottage. Just beyond this crossing came the only iron girder bridge, crossing the Muir of Ord to Tore road on a 40 feet span. The girders were of Siemens Martin's mild steel, manufactured at Dalzell Steel Works in Glasgow, and had stood tests of 28 to 31 tons of tensile strain to the square inch. The flooring was of corrugated iron made by Westwood Baillie & Co of Poplar, London. All the rivets in the girders and the flooring were of mild steel, tested to a tensile strain of 27 tons per square inch, the rivet holes being drilled rather than punched.

At Allangrange, the station serving the village of Tore, the line passed under the country road from Kessock Ferry to Conon Bridge and Dingwall before passing through more moorland and Redburn Wood where one of the steepest gradients on the line was encountered, running down

Avoch station looking towards Munlochy in Highland Railway days. Note the notice board for the North British Railway. This photograph is taken from almost the same spot as that on page 108 which shows the building converted into a house. (*Avoch Heritage Association*)

across the Little Burn, towards Munlochy. Approaching Munlochy there were broad fields to the left and to the right rolling heights rising to Ord Hill, 633 feet in height overlooking the Moray Firth. Before arriving at the station the line crossed Munlochy Burn on a 52 feet high embankment through which was a large culvert for the stream. As the ground was soft at this point piling to a depth of 16 feet was necessary. Munlochy was, and still is, a pretty village, completely sheltered from the north, east and west in the valley lying below the new station, and boasting an inn, a Free Church, a bank, a doctor, a public school and a post office, all of which remain to this day, plus a company of the Rifle Volunteers which is no longer in existence.

On leaving Munlochy station the line passed through a cutting which had provided interesting specimens of water-worn and ice-scratched boulders during excavations. On emerging from the cutting

The bridge carrying the line over the Avoch Burn still remains, complete with the reinforcing brick arch put in when it was built. (*Jack Kernahan*)

the picturesque Bay of Munlochy came into view on the right, with the rugged hills of Drumderfit and Craigiehowe on the south and the gentle slopes of Ord Hill and Lady Hill, covered with dark waving pines, to the north of the bay. Even the distant conical peaks of the hills of Strathglass and Strathconan were visible beyond Gallowhill to the south. About half a mile east of Munlochy station was the famous old red sandstone quarry at Suddie from which stone had been extracted to build Fort George, and a mile further on, to the left, could be seen the ruins of Suddie Church, the Gaelic of Suddie meaning 'a pleasant place to settle in'.

Immediately following, on the left, came into view the magnificent mansion of Rosehaugh House, residence of James Douglas Fletcher. The first passengers on the line would see that extensive additions were being made at that time, but there is no evidence of this today, the house having been razed to the ground in 1959. Mr Fletcher's late father, who had been heavily involved in the original attempts to bring the railway to the Black Isle, had also made great sanitary improvements to the next village on the line, Avoch, 'transforming it from one of the most slovenly and filthy into one of the most tidy and clean fishing villages to be found anywhere', according to the Report of the Inspector of the Board of Supervision. In addition to fishing, a prosperous woollen mill plus work on the Rosehaugh Estate formed the basis of employment for most of the villagers. The village also had a school, several churches, a post and telegraph office and a branch of the Caledonian Bank.

On leaving Avoch station the line crossed Avoch Burn on a bridge 40 feet in height. The bridge was unusual in that at its base, about five feet above the water level of the burn, there was a reinforcing brick arch. The line then passed behind the church, before going on to the final section to Fortrose, which gave probably the finest views on the route. Situated at a height of 150 feet above sea level the railway ran along the top of Craig Wood, providing spectacular views across the Moray Firth, and the stretch of water west of Fort George then known as the Firth of Inverness. Four counties (Inverness, Nairn, Moray and Banff) were visible as well as Ross and Cromarty itself. To the south views were as far as Cairngorm and the Grampians, while to the west lay Inverness and the Caledonian Canal. It was even claimed that on a clear

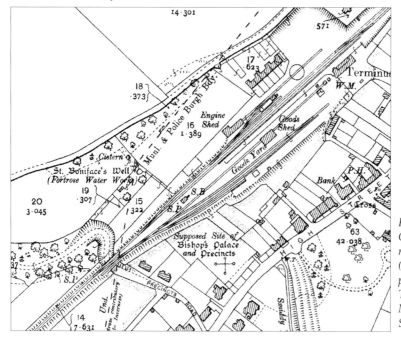

Fortrose from the Ordnance Survey map of 1905. (Reproduced with permission of the Trustees of the National Library of Scotland.)

Fortrose in the latter years of the Highland Railway, showing how the station was situated in the centre of the town. Chanonry Point can be seen in the distance. *(Highland Railway Society)*

day Ben Nevis, seventy miles distant, could be made out. Closer to the line as it approached the terminus could be seen Chanonry Point with its lighthouse and immediately opposite the firth from there the distinctive outline of Fort George. The steep gullies formed by the Redgowan and Craig Burns close to Fortrose had to be carefully infilled to form substantial embankments, the rivers flowing through on culverts deep below the level of the railway.

Great things were expected for Fortrose with the coming of the railway. It was confidently assumed that large numbers of tourists would be attracted to the town, which was well known as a watering place, with a bathing beach and magnificently situated golf course (membership five shillings per annum) and its ancient cathedral. Direct services in the season between Strathpeffer and Fortrose were contemplated. A special booklet, *Illustrated Guide to the Black Isle Railway* was published. Written by Angus J Beaton it was somewhat biased towards the geology of the area, being dedicated to the memory of Hugh Miller, the pioneer of geology who came from Cromarty. Included in the guide book were suggestions for five different walks from Fortrose station ranging from 8 to 13 miles in length, one of which involved crossing on the ferry from Chanonry Point to visit Fort George and Ardersier village. The advertisements show

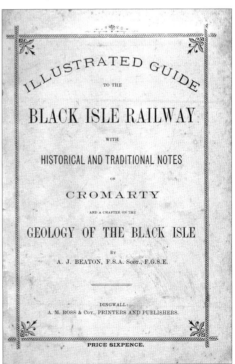

Front cover of the Guide to the Black Isle Railway *published as a guide book to the area on the opening of the branch.*

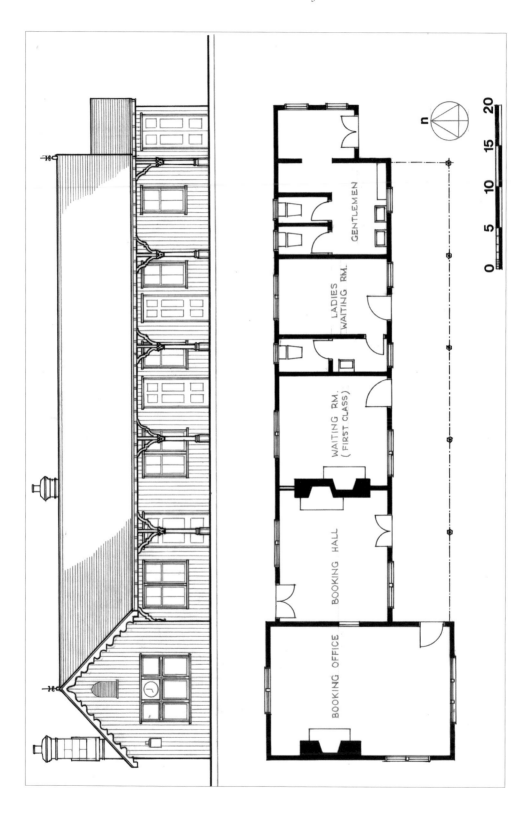

The Highland Railway built several stations to a common design in the 1890s, as illustrated in these drawing of Plockton which was similar to all the intermediate stations on the Black Isle branch. Fortrose was larger having an additional wing. It was of a similar design to Carr Bridge on the Highland Main Line, which is still in existence.

(Henry Orbach/Highland Railway Society collection)

that the railway had an immediate influence. Avoch had, and still has, a 'Station Hotel', while in Fortrose the Royal Hotel, established in 1700, became the Royal Station Hotel. John Macleod, baker and confectioner, with his tea and coffee rooms and manufacturer of 'Macleod's Famed Wine Biscuits', now traded in Station Road and like the Royal Station Hotel, advertised that he was only within one minute's walk of the railway station. Peter Grant of the Caledonian Bank advertised that eligible sites for building were now being feued on the estate of Flowerburn in the immediate vicinity of Fortrose and Rosemarkie, many commanding picturesque and extensive views and admirably situated for villas or sea bathing quarters.

The line opened for traffic on Thursday 1st February 1894, two days after the formal inspection, with the first train being the 7.15 am from Muir of Ord, returning at 8.5 am from Fortrose. The 7.15 was allowed 35 minutes for the journey, the return service being allowed 40 minutes. The trains ran with no difficulties and a service of four trains per day was offered during the first month. As 1st February was a Fast Day holiday in Fortrose, the celebrations were not held until the following day, when a public banquet was given by the Town Council and leading citizens in the Drill Hall. Most of the guests arrived by a special train of saloon carriages supplied free by the Highland Railway. Despite the heavy rain in the morning there was general rejoicing along the route, evidenced by the display of flags especially at Avoch. The guests were met on the platform by Mr Fletcher of Rosehaugh, who was to chair the event in the unavoidable absence due to the delicate state of his health of Eneas Mackintosh, Chairman of the Highland Railway, Provost Grant and Bailie Geddie and other members of the Town Council. The report of the banquet listed 132 gentlemen from the Black Isle and beyond, and there were many others not named. The hall was crowded to its utmost limits. There would appear to have been no ladies present!

After dinner, which, despite the unexpected and overcrowded attendance, was well served, the speeches began. The Queen, inevitably, was first, after which the Navy, Army and Reserve Forces were toasted and replied to, before Mr Fletcher rose to talk on 'The Resources of the Black Isle'. His speech started :-

I am sure, gentlemen, that I express your wishes when I say that we are very grateful to the directors and the shareholders of the Highland Railway for conferring upon us, who live in the Black Isle, the great boon of a railway.

This brought cheers from the audience, but it is likely that in the minds of many of the directors and officials of the Highland Railway, as well as Mr Fletcher himself, was the degree of opposition put forward by Mr Fletcher less than five years previously! What was probably not known to the audience was that Mr Fletcher had already been promised the next available seat on the Highland Railway board of directors. In his speech he went on to cite the great progress which had been made in transport in the nineteenth century. During the first decade the first public coach ran north of Perth, the journey to Inverness taking over two days. Since the first Highland train ran, less than half a century ago, the Highlands of Scotland had been revolutionised. The Black Isle had been to the forefront when the new system of husbandry was introduced into Scotland, but farms had to be let and prices accepted at lower levels due to the distance from a railway station. But now no farmer in the Black Isle could have just cause for complaint on the grounds of lack of communication with the outside world. Rosemarkie beach and the golf course were commended with the hope that these sources alone would bring a great amount of wealth to the inhabitants of the combined burghs. To applause he hoped that the day was not too far distant when the line would be extended to Cromarty.

Andrew Dougall replied for the Highland Railway. He exhorted the audience to build more houses suitable for summer occupation, suggesting that if the sun did shine at all, it always shone on Fortrose! A service of four trains per day was to be provided and if experience justified more the company would not hesitate to put them on. They would be happy to give best consideration to any suggestion for improvement of the service. On behalf of the Highland Railway he thanked Mr Fletcher for his assistance in the construction, both in giving land on very reasonable terms and being most considerate in the question of accommodating works on the Rosehaugh Estate, giving the contractors every facility.

Mr Thomson, Goods Manager, then proposed the Town and Trade of Fortrose. He mentioned that the days of opposition to railways had long gone by. Years ago if Mr Paterson and his assistants had gone out to survey a new railway he would have had the farmers setting their dogs upon him and the proprietors coming out with their guns! Now every hamlet in the country clamoured for a railway! There were a further twenty speeches, several commending the future extension to Cromarty. Andrew Dougall, deputising for the Highland Railway chairman, mentioned that he (Dougall) had come north in 1855, nearly forty years previously, to manage a 15 mile railway from Inverness to Nairn with annual revenue of £7,000. The Highland Railway now had about 450 miles, soon to increase to 500, and annual income of

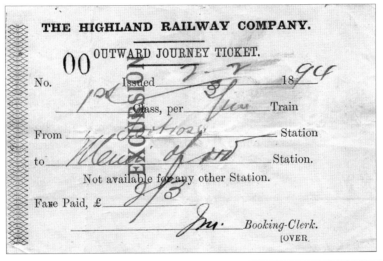

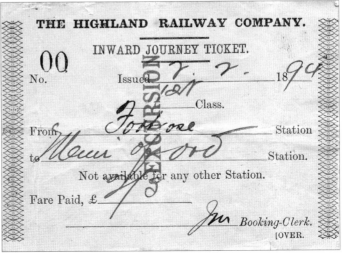

The first tickets (numbered 00) issued from Fortrose for the special excursion to Muir of Ord on 2nd February 1894. The train was the return of the special which brought guests for the celebratory opening banquet.

(Groam House Museum)

around £500,000. Murdoch Paterson, the engineer, thanked his young assistant Murdoch Macdonald who had done all the work in a most praiseworthy manner, bearing the heat of the day in summer and the cold and storms of winter. His ability predicted for him a distinguished and prosperous career. (This was true. Sir Murdoch Macdonald was later Member of Parliament for Inverness for 28 years and founder of an international engineering consultancy.) John Ross, the contractor, in response to his health being proposed, gave a very short reply, remarking that he would rather make a railway than a speech! Finally the afternoon came to an end, probably dictated by the fact that many of the participants had to catch the last train from the new station, the 5.10 pm! The special train by which they had arrived had returned as a special for the public leaving Fortrose at 3pm.

The previous day, as the first trains arrived in Fortrose, Cromarty Town Council had resolved to send a three man deputation to meet with the Highland directors to remind them of the terms of their letter of 3rd April 1890 and to ask what steps they were taking to implement the promise made in that letter to consider favourably an extension of the line to their town. Andrew Dougall accordingly met Provost Johnstone, Bailie Thomson and Councillor Junor after the banquet. They presented a petition pointing out once more that Cromarty was the natural terminus of the line and that the railway would be the means of developing the fishing and other industries of the town, and reminded him of the terms of the 1890 letter which had indicated that if the Highland were granted permission to build their line, at that time intended to go to Chanonry Point, the directors would favourably consider the early extension of the line to Cromarty, and if it was sanctioned by Parliament they would construct it. Mr Dougall said that he could assure the gentlemen that the suggested extension would receive the careful consideration of the directors, but it was impossible for him at that time to give them any definite answer.

Fortrose prior to World War I showing part of The Fleet at anchor in the Moray Firth. In addition to the station, the goods yard and shed, the turntable and the end (no 6) of Railway Cottages can be seen.

(Courtesy Margaret Tanner)

CHAPTER 5

A HIGHLAND BRANCH LINE

The navvies and engineers who had constructed the line now left the area, but one in particular, Murdoch Macdonald, who had been the resident engineer, seems to have endeared himself to the people he met and was greatly missed. On 22nd July 1895 Hugh Chisholm, agent at Muir of Ord, wrote to Murdoch, then at Blair Atholl, asking him to come to Fortrose some day soon to have a look at the new sidings to be put into the coal bank, as he was unable to order the material without a sketch from him. The letter concluded: *I am missing you very much since you left here. I wish you well.*

John Henderson, who served as Town Clerk of Fortrose for over seventy years and was also, among several other things, factor of Rosehaugh Estate, was impressed by the twenty eight year old engineer and engaged him to undertake drainage works in the town. There were obviously some difficulties in this which, according to Henderson, were the fault of the railway. Nonetheless, no personal grudge was apparent in a private letter from him to Murdoch in which, after informing him that he had acquired 50 shares at 10/- each in a syndicate for him, he went on, with reference to the drainage work:

Confound you railway people. You are the most shuffling quibblers I ever did come across. I feel so wicked about Roberts' letter that I feel inclined not to reply to it. I wrote a very nasty one but repented and did not send it. Blast you if you are not the most despicable lot of jugglers under the sun. If I showed the letter to Fletcher he would have the whole water system burst up and the reservoir charged with dynamite. For goodness sake try to put some sense into thick heads or I will not answer for the consequences.

Despite these problems, Murdoch Macdonald was obviously highly thought of in the Black Isle and became engineer for water schemes in Avoch and Munlochy as well as Fortrose.

The Black Isle Railway became the perfect example of the country branch line. At 13 miles 45 chains it was roughly the same length as the Keith to Portessie branch, also built by John Ross, which had opened in August 1884 and the Wick & Lybster Light Railway opened in July 1903. It is likely that, if construction of the Black Isle line had been commenced after the passing of the Light Railways Act of 1896, it would have been built as a light railway, avoiding the need for fencing and having lighter construction and steeper curves than normally constructed lines. The only drawback was that speed was limited to 25 mph, or 15 mph if the locomotive was running tender first.

During the first month there were four trains per day in each direction calling at all stations, three mixed and one for passengers only, starting with the 7.15 am from Muir of Ord and finishing with the 5.10 pm from Fortrose. Trains were allowed 35 or 40 minutes for the journey. The line proved popular immediately as a month later the service had been increased to seven per day. From Muir of Ord, four were mixed, the remainder being passenger only, while in the opposite direction six were mixed with only one passenger only. During the first three months of operation the service started and ended the day at Muir of Ord, rather than

Fortrose. From May 1894 the first train of the day started from Fortrose at 7.55 am, and the last of the six daily trains arrived at Fortrose at 8.50 pm. In connection with the 11.10 am train from Fortrose, the 11.25 am train from Inverness to Wick was required to call at Muir of Ord Junction to pick up passengers from Black Isle stations who wished to travel to stations north of Dingwall, and, on Tuesdays and Fridays only, for Dingwall itself, but only if the passengers were attending Dingwall Sheriff Court. The agent at Redcastle was required to advise Muir of Ord immediately on departure of the train whether or not the Wick train required to be stopped.

The reason for the service initially being worked from the Muir of Ord end may have been delays in completing the necessary buildings required at Fortrose for staff and the engine. A 50ft turntable was available at the time the line opened, but the water tower, single road engine shed or the row of six four roomed terraced houses for the railwaymen may not have been ready in time. There was no direct road access to the houses, access being from the ramp at the booking office end of the platform, across the end of the run round loop by means of a cinder crossing and thence by a path to the turntable. From there the path used the top of the pit wall close to the garden wall of number 6. This accessed the space between the line from the coaling stage to the turntable and the front gates of the houses. Such a route was obviously somewhat dangerous, risking tripping over rails to say nothing of falling into the turntable pit, but seemed to be totally acceptable in those days.

At the turn of the century, there were 34 people living in the six houses, then known as numbers 1 to 6 Railway Terrace. The two drivers were John Guthrie, a Gaelic speaker from Kingussie, and John Shivas who came from Dumfries. Two pointsmen, or signalmen, had houses: Athole Clarke from Dyce and William Thomson, a local man born in Rosemarkie who had started work with the Highland Railway as a porter at Forres on 7th January 1889 and returned to his home area on being appointed pointsman at Fortrose on 14th November 1898. The other houses were inhabited by two other Gaelic speakers, John McGillivray, surfaceman, and John Bain, a guard, originally from Gairloch. All were married and the number of children ranged from one, John McGillivray's only son, to the eight offspring of John Bain. The surfaceman had a house only because his father had been a guard and the family was not evicted. The firemen did not live in the railway houses so must have lodged elsewhere. Simon Mackenzie, the first station master, had moved on by 1901, the agent's house being occupied by James Geddes, aged 64 and born in Bogmuir, north of Fochabers, his wife who also came from Bogmuir, and his 23 year old daughter Nellie who had followed her father into railway service as a clerkess. She had been born at Dalguise, suggesting that her father had been at that station in 1878.

In addition to the railway, there was opened within a few days a further welcome addition to the facilities at Fortrose in the form of an auction mart for the sale of livestock, operated by Messrs Petrie of the Invergordon Auction Mart. The sale ring was built close to the station and there was ample room for subsequent extension if the venture was successful. The first sale boded well, with an unexpectedly large quantity of stock put forward and satisfactory prices realised. The first animals sold were pigs, followed by over a hundred head of cattle.

Lord Thurlow resigned from the Highland Railway board in April 1894 and his place was offered to and accepted by James Douglas Fletcher, who had been the great opponent of the Highland and supporter of the Great North some four years earlier. An astute man of business, he had continued to increase the family fortune made in tea and rubber, and had recently made great improvements to Rosehaugh House. He was used to asking questions and came as a 'new broom' to the Highland boardroom. At the meeting on 2nd October 1895, for

The final train from Fortrose passing the site of Rosehaugh Halt on 14th June 1960.
(Highland Railway Society)

example, the half yearly company report was laid on the table, revised, agreed to and passed, but Mr Fletcher dissented. This was following questions he had asked regarding transactions by Andrew Dougall, the long serving and trusted Secretary and General Manager, which appeared to be falsely inflating the profits on which the payment of the dividend was based as well as other apparent financial irregularities. Fletcher formally intimated his resignation as a director, but withdrew it when a joint committee of shareholders and directors was formed to investigate his accusations. The result was Dougall's resignation, while in due course Fletcher remained as a director for many years and became chairman for a short time around the turn of the century. Around 1904 he had his own private halt, Rosehaugh, built adjacent to the easterly gate to his estate. It was a very short platform reached by a short flight of steps from the adjacent roadway.

Fortrose Town Council continued to be involved in railway politics. In 1897 the scene of confrontation moved to the Great Glen, with rival schemes to extend the Invergarry & Fort Augustus Railway along the north bank of Loch Ness to Inverness, thus providing an alternative route between Inverness and Glasgow, 14 miles 57 chains shorter than that of the Highland Railway after its direct line between Inverness and Aviemore was opened. An extension of the line within Inverness as far as the southern terminal of the Kessock Ferry was intended, and the possibility of a bridge to the Black Isle was mentioned. The support of the Town Council was sought for the new line, in opposition to the Highland Railway, the company which had kept its promise to build the railway to Fortrose. By six votes to five the Council agreed to support the Invergarry & Fort Augustus (Inverness Extension) Bill, but the line was never built. The Council did, however, support the Highland in its opposition to a further attempt by the Great North of Scotland in March 1897 to seek running powers over and to widen part of the Highland's existing lines.

Nothing was said about the failure of the Highland Railway to construct the line between Fortrose and Chanonry Point via Rosemarkie, or to develop the Fort George ferry. On 1st July 1899 the shortest branch of the Highland Railway at 1 mile 38 chains opened from what had been Fort George station on the Inverness – Keith line and which was renamed Gollanfield Junction, to a station situated in the thriving fishing village of Ardersier, or Campbelltown, which was named Fort George. This was an easy section to build, but the remaining mile and a half to the fort itself would have required a large embankment along the face of the heights to the north of the village and was never built. It is possible that the railway company unsuccessfully sought a subsidy from the War Office to complete the final section. With no line to either terminal of the ferry, the Highland Railway did nothing further about implementing the pledge given at the Parliamentary Enquiry in 1890 to develop it.

The question of Cromarty continued. On 7th March 1894 the directors read an extract minute of Cromarty Town Council regarding extending the line from Fortrose to Cromarty, the subject having been briefly discussed with Andrew Dougall at the time of the opening banquet. Nothing further happened but the question of a line to Cromarty literally took a new direction when on 1st April 1896 the directors received a deputation from the area regarding a proposal for a light railway between Dingwall and Cromarty. They returned a month later, and while the directors were sympathetic, they refused to give a clear answer on any involvement of the company in the project. However on 27th October 1897 the directors decided that the Highland Railway would undertake the construction of the line, subject to suitable terms being agreed and satisfactory guarantees given by the promoters.

The Black Isle line continued to prove popular. Encouragement for visitors to come to Fortrose was given through return fares being charged at the rate of a single fare plus a third to those attending the regatta on 29th August 1896 from Tain, Strathpeffer, Forres and intermediate stations. For the opening of the golf course at Fortrose on Wednesday 13th June 1900 only the single fare was charged for return journeys to Fortrose from all Highland Railway stations for travel outwards on Monday to Thursday 11th to 14th and return on any day up to and including the following Monday.

Although there were never regular timetabled trains on the branch on Sundays, the Highland Railway broke new ground in April 1898 by running an excursion from Inverness to Glasgow

An official Highland Railway postcard of Fortrose station, probably taken shortly after the opening, as no additional buildings on the platform are evident. Note the horse-drawn vehicles possibly awaiting the arrival of a train .   *(John Alsop collection)*

Former Caledonian Railway '812' class 0-6-0 no 57605 pauses at Corrachie for the gates to be opened while hauling a single wagon to Fortrose shortly before the closure of the line.
(N Forrest/The Transport Treasury)

for an international football match. This was extended to start from and return to Fortrose, the return journey not arriving back until 4.10 am on Sunday morning, thus incurring the wrath of the Free Synod of Ross and Cromarty for disregarding the sanctity of the Sabbath.

There were requests on both sides between the Town Council and the railway company. The railway company objected to a wooden shed near the railway cottages being used as a slaughter house, so the Town Clerk was authorised to dispose of it for £20 if he could get such a sum. The Council made a somewhat larger request of the railway company in September 1898, asking for the passenger platform at Fortrose to be covered in and that cheap fares be given to Inverness, Dingwall and Strathpeffer on Thursday afternoons and Saturdays. No improvements were made to the station, but cheap excursion fares were made available from branch stations, with a 2/- third class return available from Fortrose and Avoch to Inverness by the first two trains on Tuesdays and Fridays.

Normal fares would not be considered cheap. Between Inverness and Fortrose a third class single cost 1/6, and a return was 3/-. The first class single was double the price of the third class fare, namely 3/-, with a small discount on the return at 5/-. At this time the average weekly wage for a working man was around 30/-, and for a woman 14/-. The single fare for a large (over 4 cwt) four wheeled carriage between Fortrose and Inverness was 15/9, for a small four wheeled carriage 13/6 and for a two wheeled carriage 11/3. One horse cost 9/- for the journey, two horses 15/9 and three horses 20/3. These fares were with the carriages and horses being conveyed at owner's risk. An additional 25% was charged if they went at the company's risk.

A third class single between Fortrose and Avoch was 2½d, with the first class fare 5d. Not surprisingly, there was very little demand for first class tickets on the Black Isle trains! Reduced fares were available from Avoch for fishsellers carrying their fish for sale by hawking and available for return on the day of issue or the following day. These were issued to men or women travelling to stations on the Highland Railway, but to women only travelling to stations on the Great North of Scotland Railway. A fishseller's return ticket from Avoch to Inverness cost 1/6, half the normal fare. The normal fares did not compare favourably with those on the steamer across the Firth, where a steerage return between Fortrose and Inverness was 1/-, or 1/6 for cabin class.

There were five official level crossings for road traffic on the line, although at around twenty places there were pathways where it was acceptable for people to cross the line. Only two of the level crossings were under the charge of gatewomen formally in the employment of the railway company, those at Linnie giving access to the manse and at Corrachie for the road to the farm of that name. The other three were worked by the neighbouring farmer. Only at Linnie and Corrachie crossings, where cottages were built for the keepers, were gates provided to lie across the railway while the crossing was in use for road traffic.

The sidings at all the stations were well used for goods traffic, both incoming and outgoing. In addition two sidings were provided for short periods for the transport of timber extracted from woods near the line. The first was at Spital Wood, roughly half way between Muir of Ord and Redcastle, just on the Muir of Ord side of the 2¼ milepost. Messrs A & D F Lockhart, timber merchants from Huntly, made application on 4th March 1901 for the siding. The directors requested that Lockhart reimburse the cost of the siding, estimated at £250, less the likely redeemable value of the assets namely £100. Lockhart declined this suggestion, but agreement was eventually reached in September and the siding opened after Board of Trade inspection on 24th August. Unlike the sidings at the stations, Spital Wood siding, which was on the north side of the line, was facing to trains coming from Fortrose (up trains). It was worked by a one lever ground frame controlled by the train staff for the branch. The new connection was at the top of the 1 in 65 gradient from Muir of Ord, and the siding itself was on a 1 in 200 gradient.

Allangrange goods yard on 14th August 1948. The horsebox on the left was manhandled into position after being detached from the train rather than being shunted by the engine.   (James L Stevenson)

Avoch station in 1921. Station master James A Riach, clerkess Cathie Nairn and porter Alexander Whyte. James Riach started as clerk at Dingwall in 1902, moving to Avoch as station master on 22nd October 1920. Cathie Nairn was a temporary clerkess from 30th September 1918 to 8th April 1922, while Alexander Whyte came to Avoch on 1st July 1912. *(courtesy Groam House Museum)*

The Board of Trade initially required that the engine had to be at the lower end when working the siding. This would have meant that only trains going from Fortrose to Muir of Ord could work the traffic, but the instructions for working the siding were amended to require that wagons from Muir of Ord for the siding had to be marshalled next to the rear brake van so that while shunting was going on no wagons would be permitted to stand on the gradient of 1 in 65 falling towards Muir of Ord without an engine attached. This was acceptable to the Board of Trade. Spital Wood was under the control of the station master at Redcastle, who held the key of the cabin containing the lever frame and released it to the guard when required. All traffic for the siding was worked by the 12 noon mixed train from Fortrose or the 12.45 pm goods from Muir of Ord. The timber was fully extracted and the siding closed and uplifted in 1907. Incidentally, at that time the 12 noon from Fortrose ran as a mixed train only for the months of July and August. Before and after those months it had operated as the 11 45 am goods train. It operated as a mixed train at the request of Dingwall Town Council which had requested a passenger service between the 9.20 am and the 2 pm from Fortrose.

The second siding for timber traffic was for John Macdonald & Company at Redburn Wood, midway between Allangrange and Munlochy. Also on the north side of the branch and facing to Muir of Ord it was slightly simpler than that at Spital Wood, not having a loading bank. The signalling was similar to that at Spital Wood, and, being on the 1 in 60 gradient falling to Munlochy, could be worked only with the engine at the lower end of the train. It was formally inspected in August 1914 and was in use for less than three years. On 11th July 1917 the Way and Works Committee agreed to the siding being transferred to Midfearn with Messrs Macdonald paying all the costs.

In June 1918 plans and estimates were prepared for the extension of the sidings at Munlochy

INVERNESS AND FORTROSE SECTION.

STATIONS.		A.M	A.M.	P.M.	P.M.	P.M.
Fortrose	dep.	7 10	9 20	2 0	3 50	8 5
Avoch	,,	7 17	9 26	2 6	3 56	8 11
Munlochy	,,	7 28	9 35	2 15	4 5	8 20
Allangrange	,,	7 35	9 41	2 21	4 11	8 26
Redcastle	,,	7 41	9 47	2 27	4 17	8 32
Muir of Ord Jun.	arr.	7 50	9 55	2 35	4 25	8 40
	dep.	7 55	9 59	2 40	4 30	8 44
Beauly	arr	8 5	10 9	2 50	4 40	8 54
Clunes	,,	8 10	10 15	..	4 45	8 59
Lentran	,,	8 15	10 20	....	4 50	9 4
Bunchrew	,,	8 20	10 26	..	4 55	9 10
Clachnaharry	,,	8 28	10 35	....	5 3	9 19
Inverness	,,	8 35	10 45	3 10	5 10	9 30

STATIONS.		A.M.	A.M.	P.M.	P.M	P.M.
Inverness	dep.	8 0	10 0	2 20	5 10	8 0
Clachnaharry	,,	8 5	10 6	2 25	5 15	8 6
Bunchrew	,,	8 10	10 12	2 30	5 20	8 12
Lentran	,,	8 15	10 20	2 36	5 27	8 20
Clunes	,,	8 19	10 25	2 41	5 32	8 25
Beauly	,,	8 25	10 32	2 50	5 38	8 33
Muir of Ord Jun.	arr.	8 35	10 40	2 59	5 45	8 43
	dep.	8 38	10 43	3 2	5 48	8 50
Redcastle	arr.	8 47	10 54	3 11	5 59	8 58
Allangrange	,,	8 52	11 2	3 16	6 7	9 3
Munlochy	,,	8 59	11 14	3 22	6 19	9 9
Avoch	,,	9 7	11 26	3 30	6 31	9 17
Fortrose	,,	9 12	11 32	3 35	6 37	9 25

INVERNESS AND FORTROSE SECTION.

Miles.	STATIONS.		A.M.	A.M.	P.M.	P.M.	P.M.	P.M.
	Fortrose	dep.	6 55	9 10	1 20	3 0	4 35	7 20
2½	Avoch	,,	7 2	9 17	1 27	3 6	4 43	7 26
5½	Munlochy	,,	7 14	9 26	1 39	3 15	4 55	7 35
8¼	Allangrange	,,	7 22	9 33	1 47	3 21	5 5	7 41
9¾	Redcastle	,,	7 31	9 41	1 56	3 27	5 15	7 47
13½	Muir of Ord Jun.	arr.	7 40	9 50	2 5	3 35	5 25	7 55
		dep.	7 46	9 59	2 15	4 0	..	7 58
16½	Beauly	arr.	7 53	10 9	2 24	4 9	..	8 6
19	Clunes	,,	7 58	10 15	2 29	4 14	..	8 12
20¾	Lentran	,,	8 4	10 20	2 34	4 20	..	8 20
22¾	Bunchrew	,,	8 8	10 26	2 39	4 24	..	8 25
25	Clachnaharry	,,	8 16	10 32	2 50	4 30	..	8 33
26¼	**Inverness**	,,	8 25	10 45	2 58	4 40	..	8 40

Miles.	STATIONS.		A.M.	A.M.	P.M.	P.M.	P.M.	P.M.	P.M.
	Inverness	dep.	7 45	10 0	..	*2 b 0*	2 35	4 55	8 0
1¼	Clachnaharry	,,	7 50	10 6	..	..	..	5 0	8 6
3½	Bunchrew	,,	7 56	10 12	..	..	2 46	5 10	8 12
5½	Lentran	,,	8 4	10 20	..	..	2 53	5 15	8 20
7¼	Clunes	,,	8 9	10 25	..	..	2 58	5 20	8 25
9¾	Beauly	,,	8 15	10 32	..	..	3 6	5 28	8 33
12¾	Muir of Ord Jun.	arr.	8 24	10 40		*2b23*	3 12	5 36	8 43
		dep.	8 26	10 43	*2c20*	*2b24*	3 45	5 40	8 50
16½	Redcastle	arr.	8 34	10 54	*2c28*	*2b31*	3 53	5 51	8 58
18	Allangrange	,,	8 40	11 2	*2c33*	*2b37*	3 58	6 0	9 3
20¾	Munlochy	,,	8 47	11 14	*2c39*	*2b43*	4 4	6 12	9 9
23¾	Avoch	,,	8 55	11 26	*2c47*	*2b51*	4 12	6 24	9 17
26¼	**Fortrose**	,,	9 0	11 32	*2c52*	*2b55*	4 20	6 30	9 25

b Saturdays only. *c* Saturdays excepted.

Public timetables for (above) summer 1902 and (left) summer 1909, with Inverness connecting trains.

but the work was not implemented. The sidings here were being used to capacity, as they could hold in total only 26 wagons. Redcastle could hold 28, Allangrange 44 and Avoch 30, while Fortrose goods yard had capacity for 68 wagons with a further 24 in the sidings on the north side of the line and, if required, 48 at the passenger platform. When shunting was taking place at the intermediate stations tow ropes were authorised to be used to move wagons where there was no other reasonable or practicable ways of dealing with the traffic. Wagons on down goods trains from Muir of Ord for Avoch had to be taken to Fortrose and returned to Avoch by the next available goods train.

The coming of the railway inevitably had an effect on the steamer service between Fortrose and Inverness and the Black Isle Steam Shipping Company Limited went into members' voluntary liquidation on 5th April 1898. John Henderson, Town Clerk, was appointed to act as liquidator at a fee of ten guineas. The railway did not have a monopoly on transport as

The turntable at Fortrose was always a source of fascination and a playground for children, especially those living in Railway Cottages. In 1911, possibly around the time this photograph was taken, there were 19 children living in the six cottages. (Groam House Museum)

Fortrose station in 1910 showing Kenneth Macdonald who was station master from 1907 to 1927, and a few passengers.
(Highland Railway Society)

the *Rosehaugh* remained in service between Fortrose and Inverness. On 4th October 1902, for example, she was chartered to make special runs to and from Inverness for guests attending the marriage there of Dr John Cameron of Fortrose and Miss Lilias Laverie, elder daughter of the rector of Fortrose Academy. However on 22nd November 1904, her owners, Messrs Elder & Son of Fortrose, wrote asking if the Highland Railway would consider purchasing the ship and the goodwill of their business but the offer was respectfully declined.

In the ten years between 1901 and 1911 only two of the six railway cottages changed tenants. John Guthrie the driver, William Thomson the pointsman, John McGillivray the surfaceman and John Bain the guard were still there. By this time John Bain was the father of twelve children. One had died, but seven were still living with him, making, with his wife and himself, nine occupants of the four roomed number 6 Railway Cottages, the closest to the turntable and which was always the guard's house. One of his sons, also John, started on the Highland Railway as a porter at Novar on 24th June 1911 and became a guard on 11th May 1913. The new arrivals were D Macdonald, engine driver, at number 4 and John Alexander Mackay, pointsman, at number 2. Born in Thurso, John Alex, or Jock as he was known, had been widowed in 1906 at the age of 40, but remarried the following year. A railwayman all his days, he had been at Halkirk in 1890, Golspie in 1894, Invergordon in 1896 and Fearn in 1901 before coming to Fortrose as pointsman on 11th January 1904. In addition to his new wife and two daughters by his first and one son by his second marriage, he had Kenneth Clarke, a 24 year old fireman, boarding with him. A total of 31 people lived in the six cottages, compared with 34 ten years previously. The station master in 1911 was a son of Fortrose, Kenneth Alexander Macdonald, who held the office for 20 years from 1907; he had started as goods clerk at Boat of Garten on 21st March 1898. In addition to his English born wife Charlotte Mary and their son and daughter, his wife's brother Percy Elliott, the coal agent, lived in the station house.

There were occasional staff problems. George Gammie, who had started as a clerk in the Inverness parcels office in 1900 and became station master at Allangrange on 25th May 1916, was dismissed on 21st October 1920 for intemperance. In the five years from 1912 six porters worked for only short periods at Munlochy. Donald Sutherland left honourably on 30th June 1917 for military service having been at the station for two years. Five others lasted only a few months. One left without warning, one was dispensed with as unsatisfactory, a further

The last of the ten 'Barney' 0-6-0s built by Dübs & Co, no 21, arrives at Muir of Ord with a lengthy afternoon train from Tain in 1913. Several of the passengers waiting to join may have alighted from the Black Isle train which had arrived at the other side of the island platform five minutes previously.

(Highland Railway Society)

resigned, being described as a "useless man", while two simply "disappeared". Isaac Lawrie, who had started as porter/pointsman at Struan in 1914 came to Fortrose in the same capacity on 10th December 1918 but was transferred to Stromeferry seven months later, deemed "unsatisfactory" at Fortrose as he declined to go out with a special train to a fire at Redburn.

Occasionally the Highland Railway was able to raise very small sums through granting facilities on the branch. In 1907, for example, Captain Fraser Mackenzie was granted sporting rights on the railway passing through Allangrange Estate for £1 per annum. The station master at Allangrange paid the same amount for a coal stance at his station, while £1 was also extracted from John Laing for a timber stance at Fortrose.

Prior to the First World War, a good service of trains was run. At the turn of the century

The north end of Muir of Ord station, fully signalled with Highland Railway signals. An engine is waiting in the dock platform with a train for the Black Isle branch, which leads off to the right. The down main line signal is cleared for the connecting main line train from Inverness.
(Highland Railway Society)

there were four passenger and one goods trains in each direction, calling at all stations, the passenger service effectively being two trains from Fortrose in the morning at 7.30 am and 9.20 am and two in the afternoon at 2 pm and 4 pm, returning from Muir of Ord with less than an hour's wait for shunting. The trains arrived at Muir of Ord into the branch side of the southbound island platform, giving an easy transfer for passengers into Inverness bound connections coming from the north. The engine would then be turned and shunt the coaches across the main line to the short branch departure platform dock at the end of the northbound platform, again giving an easy transfer for passengers, parcels and mail coming from trains from Inverness. On the branch all trains were worked by the same engine which was kept overnight in the small engine shed. There was at some time a shed at Muir of Ord, as in 1918 board authority was sought for an engine shed there, and on 7th April 1920 the Locomotive Committee agreed not to rebuild the shed. The ordnance survey map for 1904 shows a building behind the turntable although not described as an engine shed. A 1928 photograph of a locomotive on the turntable shows what may be small remains of this building. As the branch service operated from the Muir of Ord end for the first three months of 1894 it is possible that a shed existed there until destroyed around the time of the First World War.

All branch trains were worked by the same engine, coal and water being taken as required at Fortrose. Water was also available at Munlochy if required. The engine went to Inverness once a fortnight for a boiler washout. The 7.30 am mixed train from Fortrose collected mail at Avoch, Munlochy and Allangrange for the southbound mail train from Inverness while the following 9.20 am passenger train was allowed to take livestock traffic in piped trucks. A connecting coach left Cromarty at 10.50 am, arriving at Fortrose at 12.10 pm, passengers having to wait nearly two hours before the 2 pm train. The coach left Fortrose at 12.20 pm, arriving at Cromarty at 2 pm, passengers connecting by train for this having arrived on the mixed train due into Fortrose at 11.32 am. The 2 pm from Fortrose took mail from Cromarty off the connecting coach, as well as from Fortrose itself, Avoch and Munlochy.

By 1911 the service was similar but an evening mixed train, leaving Fortrose at 7.10 pm and returning from Muir of Ord at 8.50 pm had been added. In July 1913 the number of trains remained the same, but the 2.20 pm from Muir of Ord and 3 pm from Fortrose had been replaced with an express taking only 24 minutes for the journey, but calling at none of the intermediate stations, leaving Muir of Ord at 10 am and returning from Fortrose at 10.30 am. As the express arrived at Muir of Ord at 10.54 am and a stopping mixed train left there for Fortrose one minute later it would appear that the express service was not operated by the branch engine and coaches. The express only ran during the summer months. In October there

Built in 1893, and fitted with a Jones chimney without louvres, the last of the five 4-4-0 tanks built by Dübs & Co, nicknamed 'Yankee' tanks, no 52 was named Fortrose *for a brief period between 1901 and 1903. Numbered 15 until December 1900, it was probably the Black Isle branch engine from the opening of the line until 1903 when it was exiled to work the Invergarry & Fort Augustus Railway.*

(Highland Railway Society)

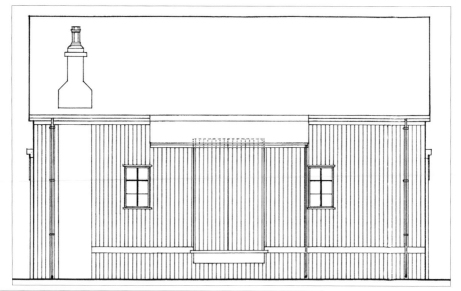

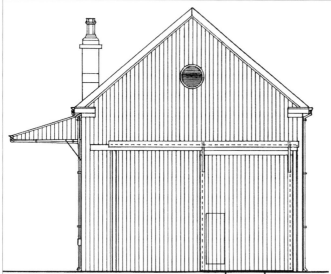

The Highland Railway had two standard designs of goods shed, one gable roofed with dressed boarding, the other with a gable roof and rough timber. The Fortrose branch stations were provided with the latter, as can be seen in some of the photographs. This drawing of Brora shed illustrates the design, although there could be variation in the dimensions; Fortrose shed was larger but still to the same basic design.
(Simon de Souza)

were three passenger, one mixed and one goods trains in the up direction and two passenger, two mixed and one goods in the down, plus an evening passenger service on Saturdays only. This continued in the early years of the war, but by the beginning of 1917 the service was reduced to three mixed trains per day, calling at all stations and taking an hour for the journey. Departure times from Fortrose were 7.10 am, 12.45pm and 4.40pm, returning from Muir of Ord at 9.50 am, 3.20 pm and 6 pm. The end of hostilities did not result in the restoration of the pre-war timetable. In 1922 there were still three mixed trains daily, taking an hour for the journey and calling at all stations. The first train did not leave Fortrose until 8.30 am, returning from Muir of Ord at 9.50 am. The first and last trains of the day were confined to general traffic from and to Fortrose only plus livestock from and to the intermediate stations. The 12.45 pm from Fortrose and 3.20 pm from Muir of Ord were to take all other traffic from all stations. If the 12.45 pm did not clear all the wagons from Redcastle, Allangrange or Munlochy, a special run of the branch train was to be made leaving Muir of Ord at 2 pm to clear the traffic, returning as quickly as possible.

It is likely that in the early years trains were operated by 'Yankee' 4-4-0 tank engines. Five of these small engines had been ordered from Dübs in Glasgow for the Uruguay Eastern Railway, which was unable to pay for them. Two had already been built and were purchased by the Highland Railway for what was considered to be a bargain price of £1,500 each. They were numbered 101 and 102. The other three were still under construction and they were completed and became numbers 11, 14 and 15, being delivered in 1893, the year before the Black Isle line opened. Given their intended destination they were soon nicknamed 'The Yankee Tanks', although this is hardly an appropriate term for South America! Numbers 11, 14 and 15 were renumbered 51, 54 and 52 respectively in 1899 and 1900. It was common Highland Railway practice to name engines after the places they served. No 52 was probably the first engine to work the Black Isle branch and was named *Fortrose* in 1901, although it had lost its name by 1903 while no 102 carried the name *Munlochy* between 1910 and 1919. The name *Rosehaugh* was given to 'Duke' class 4-4-0 no 73 in 1898, but this was in accordance with the company's policy of granting the name of a director's estate to one of the engines. It was no indication that the engine was working the Black Isle branch. No 73 had formerly been named *Thurlow* after the estate of Lord Thurlow of Dunphail, whose seat on the board was taken by James Douglas Fletcher following his resignation.

Another class of engine associated with the line was Peter Drummond's beautifully proportioned 'Small Ben' 4-4-0, his first design after appointment as locomotive superintendent to the Highland Railway in 1896. The first eight were built by Dübs & Co in 1898-99, with a further nine being built by the Highland at Lochgorm works in 1899-1901. The final three came from the North British Locomotive Co in 1906. All named, some in Gaelic, after Highland mountains, they became known as 'Small Bens' from 1908 after the arrival of the six larger boilered 'Big Bens'.

'Scrap tank' no 24, one of the three neat 0-6-0 shunting tanks reconstructed in 1903 by Drummond out of old 2-4-0 goods engines and other available parts, worked on the line

'Yankee' 4-4-0 tank no 102 operated the Black Isle branch from around 1910, when it was named Munlochy. *One of the two engines originally built to work in South America, it was given a Drummond chimney when reboilered in 1906. It is seen here awaiting departure from Fortrose.*

(Highland Railway Society)

The last of Drummond's three 0-6-0 'Scrap Tanks', rebuilt from 2-4-0 goods engines, was no 24, built in 1904. It is seen here at Munlochy with a train for Muir of Ord, probably in the first decade of the twentieth century. *(John Alsop collection)*

shortly after it was built, although it must have been hard pressed to keep time, some of the all-stations passenger services being expected to do the journey in 35 minutes.

The turntable at Fortrose was 50 feet in length while that at Muir of Ord was one inch longer and both could therefore accommodate almost all the company's engines, with the exception of the Castle 4-6-0s. Due to the length of the branch it seems likely that bunker first running by tank engines was avoided and the engines turned at the end of each trip. The discomfort of running tender first on tender engines would be avoided wherever possible, but the short run by the 2 pm from Muir of Ord as far as Munlochy when required to clear goods traffic would have resulted in occasional running tender or bunker first.

Several other Highland engines are likely to have worked the branch, but World War I brought strangers to the Black Isle. The war put enormous pressure on the Highland Railway with substantial traffic being worked principally to Invergordon and Thurso. The lack of skilled staff through men being away at the war added to the problems and it was necessary to borrow engines from other railways, both Scottish and English. During, and for a short time after, the war the Black Isle branch was worked by tank engines from the North Eastern and London & South Western Railways, but the most unlikely item of power came in the form of Great Western Railway steam railmotor no 45, which arrived in the Highlands from Bristol in January 1918. Built in February 1905, it had seats for 64 passengers, third class only, and was used for additional evening services at 6.40 pm and 9.15 pm from Invergordon, where it was allocated, to Dingwall from 18th February 1918, presumably to give service personnel from the naval establishment the opportunity to enjoy an evening in the Rossshire capital. It is likely that it was tried on the branch, although by this time the three daily services were all mixed rather than passenger trains. The railmotor was somewhat unreliable in the Highlands, and an offer by the Great Western to sell the unit to the Highland Railway in October 1919 was politely declined. It returned to England at the beginning of August 1920, spent three months in Swindon works recovering from its long journey, and returned to further new haunts in Gloucester and Birkenhead before being converted into a trailer in January 1928.

Fortrose in the 1900s. The locomotive is one of the three 'Scrap tanks', possibly no 24, which was built in 1904. The Free Church of Scotland has not been built, so the date must be before 1909. The agent's house can be seen in the left foreground. (Highland Railway Society)

The most unusual train to have operated on the branch was the self-contained engine and coach, known as a railmotor although worked by steam, loaned by the Great Western Railway at the end of World War I. No 45 had previously operated in Cornwall, and is seen here at Penzance before its long journey to the Highlands. (John Alsop collection)

Henry Casserley's Visit in 1928

Henry C Casserley visited the branch on 21st May 1928 when the trains were hauled by the first of David Jones' famous 'Skye Bogie' 4-4-0s, by then numbered 14277 and painted in the LMS 'Midland' red livery, complete with yellow lining and LMS crest on the cabside,

On the Muir of Ord turntable which was one inch longer than that at Fortrose. The rubble lying behind the turntable could be the remains of a building temporarily used as an engine shed.   (H C Casserley)

After being turned, 14277 is attached to its coaches at the side of the island platform on the up side at Muir of Ord, where it had earlier arrived from Fortrose.   (H C Casserley)

(Above) 14277 has now taken the branch train across to the dock platform at the north end of Muir of Ord, facilitating the transfer of passengers from the northbound 3.10 pm Inverness to Helmsdale at the main platform, hauled by 'Big Ben' 4-4-0 no 14420 Ben a'Chait *and 'Small Ben' 4-4-0 no 14404* Ben Clebrig. *The branch train will depart at 3.50pm.*

(H C Casserley)

(Right) Taken from the train near Avoch.

(H C Casserley)

(Below) At Fortrose, turned, and ready to return to Muir of Ord at 4.40pm. (H C Casserley)

Fortrose station in the early years of the LMS. The signal cabin closed on 13th July 1926. The photograph would have been taken shortly after this date, as the signals have been removed, but the cabin, subsequently taken to Rosemarkie by former pointsman Jock Mackay, is still in place.

(John Alsop collection)

'Small Ben' 4-4-0 no 14406 Ben Slioch backs on to the first train of the day, the 3.35pm, to Fortrose in the dock platform on the down side at Muir of Ord on 10th April 1946. The coach will have spent most of the day in the dock since arriving from Fortrose before 10 am. In the interim 14406 will have worked the daily goods train to Fortrose and back. It still carries the lamp code for a pick-up goods train.

(H C Casserley)

Chapter 6

LMS Days

From 1st January 1923 the Highland Railway, together with the Caledonian and the Glasgow & South Western, became part of the London Midland & Scottish Railway, which stretched from Dorset in the south to Thurso in the north. Fortrose Town Council was not slow in making an approach to the new operators of the Black Isle branch, in the hope that they might improve facilities. At the end of 1922 the line still had the service of three mixed trains per day introduced during the war time economies of 1917. On 18th January 1923 the Town Council held a special meeting to consider making an approach to the new railway company seeking their help and influence to bring Fortrose and Rosemarkie 'into repute as a watering place and health resort by affording better and quicker travelling facilities and by encouraging in any other way they might consider advisable the advent of visitors in pursuit of health or pleasure'. A suitable letter was prepared and sent to the Deputy General Manager of the LMS, Donald Matheson, formerly General Manager of the Caledonian.

On 1st March Donald Matheson and a number of LMS officials visited Fortrose where they met with the Fortrose and Rosemarkie Development Committee. They had a drive round the burgh, inspecting the golf course and the new bowling green and tennis courts. Expressing themselves as highly pleased with the advantages of Fortrose and Rosemarkie as health and pleasure resorts they promised that everything possible would be done to improve the train service and have the place properly advertised. Another letter was submitted by the Town Clerk suggesting that, in addition to improving the train service and undertaking some advertising, the LMS might consider building a hotel and extending the golf course, no doubt with the then current developments adjacent to the former Caledonian station at Gleneagles in mind.

On 20th March the LMS considered a report by Donald Matheson in which he merely suggested that in summer time the service might be somewhat improved, but beyond that in his opinion nothing more should be done. The directors approved his suggestion that he write back to the Town Clerk to the effect that the board, having considered the proposals, regretted that they did not see their way to giving effect to them.

The timetable was greatly improved from 9th July 1923. Until that date the service of three mixed trains per day had continued, leaving Fortrose at 8.30 am, 12.45 pm and 4.40 pm, each taking an hour for the journey. They returned at 9.50 am, 3.20 pm and 5.55 pm, the first and last taking 45 minutes and the middle one 54 minutes. After 9th July a goods train left Fortrose at 6.15 am, returning as a mixed train from Muir of Ord at 7.30 am. With the 1923 improvements there were four passenger services leaving Fortrose at 8.50 am, 10.30 am, 1.30 pm and 5 pm, returning at 9.45 am, 11.5 am, 3.20 pm and 5.55 pm. In addition a Saturday evening train left Fortrose at 7.30 pm returning at 8.15pm. The 5.55pm from Muir of Ord also took livestock traffic in piped cattle trucks. The branch train consisted of one composite coach, one third, and a brake van. If the first trains of the day did not clear wagons to or from Redcastle, Allangrange or Munlochy, as in pre-1917 Highland Railway days, a special run of the branch train was

PLEASE RETAIN THIS BILL FOR REFERENCE.

B 439 R

CHEAP

EVENING EXCURSION

ON

WEDNESDAY, 27th JUNE, 1934

BY SPECIAL EXPRESS TRAIN

TO

FORTROSE

				p.m.
INVERNESS	...	...	... leave	6 10
FORTROSE	...	...	... arrive	7 0

*The RETURN TRAIN leaves FORTROSE at 10.15 p.m.,
and arrives INVERNESS at 11.5 p.m.*

1/- RETURN FARE 1/-

The Tickets are valid by the Special Train in each direction on Day of Issue only.

Children under three years of age, free; three years and under fourteen, half fare.

CONDITIONS OF ISSUE OF EXCURSION AND OTHER REDUCED FARE TICKETS.—These Tickets are issued subject to the Notices and Conditions shown in the Company's Time Tables. For luggage allowances also see Time Tables.

All information regarding Excursions and Cheap Fares and all Railway Travel and Transport can be obtained at L M S Stations or from Mr T. Johnstone, District Goods and Passenger Manager, Inverness.

June, 1934.

J. BALLANTYNE, *Chief Officer for Scotland.*

E.R.O. 53302.

CHRONICLE, INVERNESS.

Fireman Jack Mackenzie at Redcastle. He was a fireman on the branch from 1922, his driver normally being Charlie Taylor. While at Fortrose he became a passed fireman and moved to Inverness in 1940. Behind him can be seen the goods shed which was moved to Beauly to replace the one there destroyed by fire in 1924. *(Courtesy John MacKenzie)*

made from Muir of Ord at 2.20 pm. As indicated by Donald Matheson in his report, this excellent service lasted only until the end of September. Thereafter the branch returned to having only three mixed trains daily, with no Saturday evening excursion services.

A few changes were made on the line. The first was unplanned and arose due to the goods shed and office at Beauly being destroyed by fire on 8th April 1924. A fixed crane and weighing machine were also destroyed. The value of goods mineral and livestock traffic at Beauly was around £10,000 per annum and there was keen road motor transport competition in the area. As the goods shed at Redcastle was in good condition, and had a goods platform and verandah and a 30 cwt hand crane, it was dismantled and transferred to Beauly, but erected in a different location from the one destroyed. With some track alteration this gave an increase in the capacity for wagon discharge, from 26 to 39, as the goods yard could be filled to capacity particularly in spring time. A saving of £100 per annum in engine time was anticipated. At Redcastle there was a small store on the platform used for accommodating road van goods. This store was separated from the left luggage office by a partition. As the left luggage traffic was negligible, the partition was removed and the enlarged space used for goods traffic. A loading bank was formed at the Fortrose end of the platform to enable carts to load heavy articles. The cost of the work was £1,496.

At Fortrose the LMS decided that there was no need for a signal cabin with full signalling, so the cabin was formally closed with effect from 13th July 1926. Telegraphic block working was thereafter abolished, the line continuing to be worked under 'one engine in steam' regulations with a train staff. The running line signals were removed and points worked from an elevated three lever ground frame. There remained Highland Railway style ground shunting signals at Fortrose and the intermediate stations controlling the exits on to the main line from the goods yard. These had also been provided at the temporary sidings at Spital Wood and Redburn Wood in Highland Railway days.

John Alick (Jock) Mackay came to Fortrose as a pointsman (signalman) on 11th January 1904, but by the time the signal cabin closed he had become a porter/guard. At the time living in Rosemarkie, some five months before the cabin closed he purchased a small plot of ground at the foot of his garden and in due course erected on it a building which incorporated the Fortrose signal cabin and another small building of Highland railway origin. The LMS recorded an estimated recovery value for the cabin of £45, compared with the original cost of £160. The building, known as 'The Cabin', was used as temporary accommodation for his family while works were carried out in his house, but in the 1940s he and his second wife moved permanently into his adapted former workplace. He lived there until his death, aged 82, in 1948 and his wife Isabella Rose remained there until her death in 1962.

On 24th April 1943 a number of the inhabitants of the Killearnan parish gathered at the station master's house at Redcastle to mark the occasion of the retirement of Alexander Holm as station master and postmaster, posts which he had held for nearly thirty five years. He had started his railway career at The Mound as clerk on 3rd January 1893 and was at Redcastle from 16th December 1908. The local post offices at Killearnan and Tore had been transferred to the stations at Redcastle and Allangrange respectively when the line had opened in 1894. Mr Holm was praised for the remarkable tact, courtesy and geniality shown to everyone in the performance of his onerous duties and was presented with a wallet of treasury notes. Mrs Holm received a handsome and valuable silver entree dish. The company was thereafter hospitably entertained by Mr and Mrs Holm.

Alexander Holm, station master, at Redcastle. He retired in 1943, after fifty years' service with the Highland Railway, having been in charge of both the station and the post office at Redcastle since December 1908.
(Holm Family, courtesy Alasdair Cameron)

At the beginning of the war the station master at Fortrose was John Oliver. He moved shortly after the war started and by 1947 he was at Aviemore. As with his predecessor in 1901, James Geddes, John Oliver's daughter Georgina (Georgie) followed her father into railway service as a clerkess, and in the late 1960s was at Maxwell Park on Glasgow's Cathcart Circle.

While men were called up for war service clerkesses were employed at Fortrose, although they were not the first ladies to work on the line. Cathie Nairn had been clerkess at Avoch in late Highland Railway days. At Fortrose Margaret Smith was passenger clerkess and Molly Cherry goods clerkess. Margaret's railway career had started in Inverness. For two years she cycled daily from her home in Avoch to North Kessock where she left her bike before taking the ferry across the firth and then a bus to the town centre. Life was a lot easier when she was offered the post of clerkess at Fortrose, only two miles from home. The other staff at Fortrose during the war were James Dick, station master, who had started with the Highland Railway as clerk at Invershin on 24th April 1913, Frankie Hay and Frank Thomson, drivers, Jimmy Leitch and Jack Fraser, firemen, Ephie Sinclair, Jock Gordon and Jim MacBain, guards and Alec Urquhart, goods guard/porter. Jock Mackay had retired by this time, probably in the early 1930s. Romance blossomed at the station. In 1944, the year after he arrived at Fortrose, Jimmy Leitch married Frankie Hay's daughter Betty and in 1946 Jock Gordon married Molly Cherry.

Due to an overturned oil lamp, the wooden single road engine shed at Fortrose was burned to the ground in spring 1943, unfortunately when it was occupied by 'Small Ben' 4-4-0 no 14416 *Ben a'Bhuird*, which had to be sent to St Rollox for repainting. The Lybster branch closed in 1944, and consideration was given in January 1945 to transferring the shed to Fortrose, but nothing came of this. Local enterprise had already resulted in the speedy construction of a corrugated iron replacement shed, looking somewhat like an overgrown garage, but incorporating the original smoke pot and the front circular ventilator salvaged from the destroyed shed, although the latter

'Loch' class 4-4-0 no 14381 Loch Ericht at the original engine shed at Fortrose, on 24th September 1935. The shed was destroyed by fire in 1943.
(Highland Railway Society)

was put in at a 90 degree angle to the way in which it had been built in the original.

In the mid-1920s there was a landslip on the north side of the line in the cutting between Avoch and Fortrose near the 12¼ milepost. Around 30 feet of the fencing became undermined and with the concurrence of Rosehaugh Estate a temporary fence was erected. By the end of 1929 there was danger of a further slip occurring as the cutting was through running sand and crumbling rock. The Estate was also requesting that the fence be set back. The solution was that the relevant area of ground comprising 105 square yards be purchased from the Estate for £15. The normal speed limit on the branch was 40 mph, reduced to 20 mph on the tight curve at Muir of Ord, but near the landslip area only 35 mph was permitted.

By the close of the 1920s the timetable comprised four passenger services from Fortrose, one non-stop, and five return services, plus the additional Saturday evening train leaving Fortrose at 8 pm, returning at 8.50 pm, so it was possible for folk from the Black Isle to enjoy a Saturday afternoon in Inverness. This was not so easy on weekdays as the last train from Muir of Ord left at 5 pm. Economies were now becoming necessary once more and two services in each direction were suspended. By 1938 there were only three passenger trains in each direction plus the Saturday evening train, but travel to Inverness on Saturday afternoons was made easier as the 1.5 pm from Fortrose ran through to Inverness while the 8.40 pm from Muir of Ord was a through train from Inverness. The return fare was 1/-. The 8 pm from Fortrose and 8.40

The first of the 'Small Ben' class 4-4-0s, LMS no 14397, formerly Highland Railway no 1, Ben y'Gloe, built in 1898, passing the replacement Fortrose engine shed after being turned.
(Highland Railway Society)

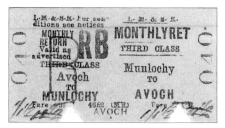

The LMS held a significant shareholding in the local bus company, Highland Omnibuses, and allowed passengers to interchange tickets, although usually a supplementary fare had to be paid to travel by train. That was often accepted, as it was often easier to carry bulky items by train. The top two tickets allowed a bus passenger to return by rail and were printed on grey background with a touch of blue. The lower two, stamped 'RB', allowed a rail passenger to return by bus, the fare being adjusted accordingly, and were printed on the green background used for third class tickets.

(Godfrey Croughton collection)

A 4-6-0 constructed for hauling heavy goods trains over the main line from Perth to Inverness seemed extravagant motive power for a two-coach branch train but by the time this photograph was taken in the late 1940s, the locomotive was well past its best, especially after wartime duty. No 57956 waits at Fortrose with an afternoon train to Muir of Ord in the late 1940s. As usual a single passenger coach sufficed, on this occasion a non-corridor one, plus a full brake for parcels and the guard. The loco must have been a tight fit on the 50ft turntable as the distance between leading bogie wheel and rear tender wheel was 46ft 8 while the overall length was 55ft 5in over buffers.   *(C L Kerr)*

pm from Muir of Ord also ran on Thursdays, the Fortrose half-day. An unusual aspect of the service, which was still apparent when passenger services ceased, was that the first train from Fortrose, which left at 9.5 am, was allowed seven minutes more for the journey on Mondays, Tuesdays and Wednesdays than on the subsequent three days. One freight train ran each day, leaving Fortrose at 10.55 am and returning at 12.10 pm, although it had to leave ten minutes earlier on Saturdays and take twelve minutes less on the journey to arrive at Fortrose in time to allow the afternoon train to Inverness to leave at 1.5 pm. The

A livestock wagon label for a consignment from Fortrose to a farm about three miles west of Muir of Ord. The printing was green with the '3' over-printed in red. (John Roake collection)

Second World War saw services reduced to worse than the previous war, with just two trains each day, leaving Fortrose at 8.45 am on Mondays, Tuesdays and Wednesdays, 9.5 am on Thursdays, Fridays and Saturdays, and 4.25 pm every day. In the opposite direction the first train was not until 3.30 pm, the second two hours later. Saturday afternoons in Inverness were still provided for with departure from Fortrose at 1.5 pm, as well as 8.5 pm, the latter to take the stock to Muir of Ord for the 9.20 pm back to Fortrose.

In addition to the timetabled trains, special freight trains were run when required, particularly in connection with animal sales, and lengthy excursion trains brought visitors to Fortrose. On Sunday 1st July 1928, for example, an excursion left Elgin at 12.30 pm, arriving at Fortrose at 2.37 pm, with an alternative of Strathpeffer at 2.32 pm. The return train left Fortrose at 6.10 pm arriving back at Elgin at 8.25 pm. The third class excursion fare was 4/6 from Elgin, or 2/3 from Inverness. The following Monday for the Inverness holiday a late return train leaving Fortrose at 8 pm was run, excursion return fares throughout the area being offered at single fare plus a third.

The normal goods traffic reflected the agricultural nature of the Black Isle, with animal feeding stuffs and the other requirements for farms being brought is, as well as domestic coal and the stocks required by the various shops in the area.

A postcard sent from Allangrange in 1910, probably relating to the return to the west coast of sheep sent to the Black Isle for wintering.
(John Roake collection)

On one of its last duties before withdrawal after a working life of 38 years, 'Clyde Bogie' 4-4-0 no 81A Colville on Fortrose turntable on 30th August 1923. Named after Lord Colville of Culross, a director of the Highland Railway, it does not appear to have been allocated, let alone carried, an LMS number, despite having survived in traffic well into 1923.   *(Highland Railway Society)*

The produce of the farms, principally potatoes, grain, sugar beet and of course animals, mainly cattle and sheep but also occasionally pigs, were taken from the stations, as well as timber felled throughout the area, which left in the form of both logs and sawn timber. The area abounded in rabbits which formed another export. In the autumn substantial numbers of sheep were brought from the west coast of Scotland and the Western Isles for wintering in the milder climate of the Black Isle, returning to their homes in the spring.

A useful facility provided by the LMS on lines with a relatively sparse service was the ability for passengers with return tickets to make the return journey by bus. Since rail fares were latterly higher than bus fares the passenger paid no more to come back by bus, but received no refund even if the first class fare had been paid, as the ticket was valid for travel by either method. It was also possible for passengers with return portions of bus tickets to exchange them for train tickets by paying a supplementary fare. From Inverness to Redcastle or Munlochy, for example, the supplement was 1/2d, while to Munlochy it was 1/7d. Visitors to Fortrose were also encouraged by the availability of two camping coaches stabled at the end of the line beyond the run round loop opposite the station.

As the timetable changed, so did the hours of duty for the staff. While the 1923 timetable improvements would have been greatly appreciated by the passengers, the fact that the first train leaving Fortrose from 9th July 1923 was the 6.15 am goods, compared with the 8.30 am mixed before that change, the engine crews had to have a much earlier rise. The previous timetable, commencing at 8.30 am and finishing at 6.40 pm, may well have been worked by a single set of men, but two shifts would be needed for the new service.

Muir of Ord and Fortrose.

Mls			a.m	a.m	p.m		p.m		F
	Muir of Ord	lev.	7 55	10 5	3 25	—	5 40	—	8p52
3¾	Redcastle . . .		8 7	1013	3 33	.	5 48	—	9 0
5½	Allangrange — —		8 15	1018	3 38	—	5 53	—	9 5
8	Munlochy . . .		8 27	1023	3 43	—	5 58	—	9 10
11¼	Avoch — — —		8 40	1029	3 49	—	6 4	—	9 16
13½	Fortrose .	arr.	8 47	1035	3 55	.	6 10	.	9 22

		a.m	H	R	SO	SX	p.m	F
Fortrose	lev.	7 0	9 a 5	9 a 5	1 p 5	1p15	4 40	8p 0	—
Avoch		7 6	9 11	9 13	1 11	1 21	4 46	8 6	.
Munlochy — —		7d13	9 18	9 22	1 18	1 28	4 53	8 12	—
Allangrange .		7d19	9 24	9 30	1 24	1 34	4 59	8 17	.
Redcastle — —		7d24	9 31	9 38	1 31	1 41	5 6	8 23	.
Muir of Ord	arr.	7 30	9 40	9 47	1 40	1 50	5 15	8 31	.

Summer 1939 public timetable. The evening trains ran on Thursdays and Saturdays only.

During the late 1930s the Railway Terrace houses were occupied by driver Charlie Taylor (no 1), fireman Jack Mackenzie (no 2), passenger guard Jim MacBain (no 3), driver Frank Hay (no 4), Jim McGillivray, possibly a permanent way inspector working from Muir of Ord, (no 5) and guard Jock Skinner (no 6). The only name listed which had been there at the beginning of the century was McGillivray. Jim's father John had been in house number 5 in 1901. Jock Skinner had one of his hands damaged in a shunting accident when it was squeezed between wagon buffers.

The 'Yankee' tanks which had served the branch well in its first years were scrapped by the LMS between 1924 and 1934, and during LMS days 'Small Bens' were most likely the normal branch engines, but 'Strath', 'Loch', and 'Skye Bogie' 4-4-0s were also to be found as well as 'Barney' 0-6-0s. In the first year of the LMS, still wearing Highland Railway livery which it was destined never to lose as it was withdrawn the following year, the line was worked by one of the last of the 1886 'Clyde Bogies', no 81A *Colville*, named after Lord Colville of Culross, appointed a director of the Highland Railway in 1885, the year before the engine was built. This was undoubtedly one of the engine's last duties, with many of the older engines found on the Black Isle line spending their more glorious days on the main Highland lines.

In 1939 five of Sir William Stanier's 2-6-2 tanks introduced in 1935, nos 185 to 189, were sent to Blair Atholl, principally to be used for banking duties on the steep climb to Druimuachdar Summit. They must have been tried out on other lines, as in late 1939 one appeared on the Fortrose branch. Despite being a tank engine it was turned on the turntable, but on its first day on the branch it became derailed at Muir of Ord, as the turntable was not properly aligned and the front bogie dropped over the edge of the pit. Matters were resolved fairly quickly, but the train ran somewhat later than the timetable, and the tank did not last very long at Fortrose. The following year it and its class fellows were to be found at Dawsholm shed in Glasgow, working on the Glasgow Central Low Level lines, far from the pure air of the Black Isle!

A typical train in LMS days at Fortrose waiting to depart for Muir of Ord. The locomotive is a former Highland one, no 14409 Ben Alisky, *but the coaches, one from the London & North Western Railway and the other Lancashire & Yorkshire, were among those sent north by the LMS to replace ageing Highland vehicles.* (C L Kerr)

JAMES STEVENSON'S VISIT IN 1948

James L Stevenson visited the branch on 14th August 1948, photographing each station from the train, which was hauled by Small Ben 4-4-0 no 14399 *Ben Wyvis*.

Redcastle station, looking towards Muir of Ord. *(James L Stevenson)*

Allangrange station, looking towards Muir of Ord. *(James L Stevenson)*

Munlochy station, looking towards Fortrose.   *(James L Stevenson)*

Avoch station, looking towards Fortrose.   *(James L Stevenson)*

The coaches at the platform at Fortrose while 14399 is turned.   *(James L Stevenson)*

14399 by the water tower at Fortrose.   *(James L Stevenson)*

14399 at the head of the train at Fortrose ready to return with the 4.25pm to Muir of Ord. Passengers had the choice of an elderly Highland bogie coach or a 1930s LMS coach which could be found in express trains of that period. (James L Stevenson)

Not many photographs were taken showing the side of the station building away from the platform. James Stevenson did not have a chance during his trip in 1948, but 40 years later his son was able to capture the road approach to Redcastle. Somehow the building had survived when others disappeared and is still in use today, much renovated, as a training centre. It even served as the local post office for a time. (Hamish Stevenson)

The final train on the line in June 1960 provided many enthusiasts with their first and only opportunity to travel over the branch. Many photographs were taken of the train, but this one of Munlochy is of interest as it shows the road side view of the station, which at that time was in remarkably good condition. The paintwork looks quite new.   (Harold Bowtell/HRS collection)

For much of its almost fifty year life 'Small Ben' 4-4-0 no 14409 Ben Alisky ran with a bogie tender, having exchanged with 'Barney' 0-6-0 no 134 in 1909. This added 3½ ft to the length, giving 47ft 7½ in, a neat fit on the 50ft turntable at Fortrose.   (Highland Railway Society)

CHAPTER 7

REMINISCENCES

Despite the fact that passenger services were withdrawn as long ago as 1951 there are several people still alive, and many who have passed on, who have recorded their memories of the Black Isle Railway.

The stations were centres of the communities and many friendships were made on the train. In the 1920s and 30s there were few cars and the railway was still a lifeline, despite for some years the relatively poor service. Just about everything needed in the district came by train until the Second World War. Fortrose was very dependent on the train. Some people had bicycles while others had a pony and trap. Children would wait for hours to see if Mr Fletcher from Rosehaugh would pass in his car. Even in the early 1940s there were only two cars in Avoch.

The drivers and the firemen cleaned and looked after the engine, or occasionally the two engines, and kept them spotless and shining. They looked particularly smart in the deep crimson livery of the LMS, as they had in the dark green Highland Railway livery before 1923. The porters looked after the coaches, which in early days were somewhat spartan and lacked heating but latterly were well upholstered, keeping them clean and taking a real pride in their work. The carriages were mostly elderly and had served on the main lines in their prime but, on being superseded by more modern vehicles, were put out to serve their last years on the branch lines; they were described as 'basic but adequate'. First class was offered, but hardly anyone ever used it. Children gazed through the windows, but wouldn't dream of entering a first class compartment, and it was a rare event for a first class ticket to be sold on the branch.

The children, several of whom had 3 monthly season tickets for travelling to Dingwall in the days when the service enabled such a journey to be possible, were somewhat terrified of Jock Mackay, the guard who had formerly been the signalman. Saturday was the big day, when it was possible for a shilling to go into Inverness, sometimes to 'the pictures', returning on the evening train, which would often be met by crowds at each station. There would occasionally be music and a sing-song while waiting for the train.

One youngster who started his working life at Munlochy station remembered horses and carts waiting to get into the sidings to take arriving loads of feed and fertilisers to the farms as well as coal which was usually bought by the wagon load. Coal was also needed for the steam engines used at the threshing mills. Oats and barley from James Dingwall, grain merchant at Culbokie, would be despatched, sometimes destined for as far as Stornoway. Cattle, sheep and pigs were regularly sent from Munlochy and other goods loaded were vegetables, corn and potatoes which when necessary were covered in straw for protection against frost. Angus Cameron was the coal merchant and Hugh Fraser from the garage did most of the carting.

The steepest gradient on the line was 1 in 60. This was found on the climb out of Fortrose, which could be very difficult on a cold start with a heavily loaded train, and for two miles from Munlochy to Allangrange. Trees overhanging the track could make the rails slippery

A wagon label, probably for a wagon being sent empty to Munlochy for timber to be despatched by John Macdonald & Son, who had their own siding at Redburn Wood between Munlochy and Allangrange during World War I.

(John Roake collection)

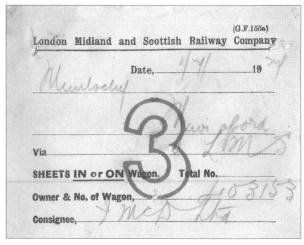

at Fortrose so it was necessary to ensure that the engine had full sandboxes as well as being fully coaled and watered. The sanding equipment on older engines was not particularly efficient and it was often difficult to get going from Fortrose with a heavy train of timber or livestock. Occasionally trains ran back towards Avoch from Munlochy to take a run at the incline up past Drummore farm. If this failed, the train had to be split, with half left at Munlochy, the first half being taken to Allangrange with the engine returning to Munlochy to collect the other half which was then coupled to the first half at Allangrange to proceed on its way. If the weather was dry the sparks from the engines would set fire to the woodlands in the Allangrange Estate and the railway staff had to do their best to extinguish the fires.

Timber was a regular item handled at Fortrose and Allangrange, much of it destined for use as pit props in the coal mines. Forestry Commission lorries had second men to help the driver with the loading and packing which was all done by hand. Timber was roped into the wagons by the station staff. Wagons brought in coal for the merchants in Fortrose and one who came from Cromarty. The wagons were then filled with the timber, although often there was such a large quantity of timber that empty wagons had to be brought in. The engines, of course, had to be fully coaled every day. A light load and an engine going at speed had a very useful benefit for the people along the line. The coal easily fell off the tender! It was not unknown for people to go along the line with buckets, filling them with the coal.

A group of ladies preparing to depart from Fortrose for a day out.

(Groam House Museum)

The water tower at Fortrose, close to cottage number 4, occasionally had a secondary, if unauthorised, use. During the 1920s there were sometimes problems with the town water supply, possibly going back to the days of the construction of the railway. The water for the town had to be turned off, so the town crier went round informing people of this. The railway water tower formed an ideal source of supply in the circumstances!

The turntable was a source of endless fascination for children, who would be allowed to help turn the engine and would enjoy standing on the turntable to 'get a hurl'. The guard's van was another mysterious place, full of mail, newspapers, parcels and even smaller items of livestock such as chickens. There was, as expected, a great degree of flexibility in running the railway. If the driver saw someone running for the train he would happily wait. "Just tell Frankie Hay I'm coming" was a frequent request to a faster fellow passenger on the way to the station. Depending on whom you were and who the driver was the train would stop between stations for passengers if required. Fortrose was a long way from railway headquarters in Glasgow or London in LMS days, and even from Inverness!

The station was also, of course, a place of sadness on the occasion of departures. When a young person was leaving the villages for university, or to train as a nurse, the whole village turned out to wish them well, with presents of chocolates and flowers and the local minister giving a prayer and a blessing.

Elma Cameron had many memories of her father's time as station master at Redcastle. Alexander Holm came to Redcastle as station master on 16th December 1908. Having a post office, it was always a busy place, and the social centre of the area. The post office was open from 9 am to 7pm and from 9 am to 10 am on a Sunday. The postal business was carried out in the back room which contained a large dresser where all the sorting and stamping was done.

Redcastle station in 1908. Station master James Morrison (right) and porter John Mackintosh. James Morrison moved to Avoch in December 1908 (see page 37) and then in February 1911 to Conon. Before coming to Redcastle he had been the first station master at Invergarry when it opened in July 1903. John Mackintosh started as porter at Redcastle on 9th May 1908. (SRPS/Iain Morrison collection)

Sack hire was an important part of railway business at Redcastle, continuing into the 1950s. This invoice was raised in the first few weeks of the LMSR.

(John Roake collection)

Friday was pension day, while benefits for widows and orphans were paid on Tuesdays. All the war news came in on the 'ticker', the morse code telegraph system, and Mr Holm wrote out the news and posted it on the back window. After the war there were between 70 and 80 pensioners receiving 10/- per week and several others receiving 5/- for having lost sons or brothers in the war.

On Saturday night there would be a large gathering at Fortrose waiting for the delivery of the *Football Times* on the last train at 9 pm. This newspaper was very popular because it contained a column called the 'Chirpings' written by a railway surfaceman from Beauly known as the 'Gutter Sparrow'. It contained lots of interesting snippets of local gossip.

In winter time the children used to like to stand on the platform opposite the engine when the 5 o'clock train arrived in the darkness. The fireman would be shovelling coal into the firebox and the heat was very welcome! The train always waited for five minutes at Redcastle. The driver, either Jimmy Smith or Frank Hay, would spend the time polishing the engine. At the back of the station buildings there was a railway weighbridge for weighing cartloads of coal and other goods. All the farmers bought coal for themselves and their men by the wagonload. Potatoes, coals, sticks and oatmeal were the perks for ploughmen, making up for their meagre pay. Railwaymen got their coals at a cheap rate, which was weighed out at the station for the porter, the two surfacemen and the station house.

Young pigs and calves arrived tied in bags in the guard's van. On one occasion Mr Holm was bitten by a young pig on the thumb which became septic. Another injury occurred when the porter, helping with loading of livestock, lost his hold on the heavy gate and dropped it on the station master's toe! John Mackintosh the porter would amuse the children by sitting them on his knee and drawing pigs with curly tails. He smelt of tarry rope, used for tying the wagons of barley, oats, potatoes and bales of straw, mostly for Hendersons of Dingwall. The railway was the only form of transport in those days. When a horse wagon arrived the children would play on it at the loading bank, as there was a compartment at one end for the attendant. The goods shed was also a marvellous place for play before it was transferred to Beauly in 1924. There was a lovely smell in the lamp room, half way down the platform, where the porter filled and polished the oil lamps. There was a lamp at each end of Mr Holm's desk, another in the post office, one at either end of the platform and one down by the signal which stood at the Muir of Ord end of the platform; this was the only signal on the branch, other than ground shunting signals and fixed distants at the level crossings, after the closure of Fortrose signal cabin in 1926.

A flat sort of estate wagon came up from the castle at Redcastle loaded with fruit and vegetables from Baroness Burton's gardens. This produce would be for Dochfour Estate which the Baroness let for shooting parties every year. One big event which took place every February was the transport of bulls from Garguston farm to the Perth sales. The farm had a well known herd of Shorthorns and on the day a procession of bulls came slowly along the road to the station. Big casks of 'porter' and bags of locust beans came in each year as special feed for the animals.

Redcastle's big day came in the early 1920s when the then Prince of Wales, later King Edward VIII and Duke of Windsor, came for a shooting weekend at the castle. Huge amounts of provisions arrived and on the day before he arrived large numbers of trunks and cases.

During the Second World War the castle at Redcastle was commandeered by the RAF and bombs were brought in by goods train and deposited in the woods around Kilcoy. This was a dispersal policy so that there was no great concentration of bombs in one place.

John Mackenzie lived in no 2 Railway Cottages in Fortrose during the 1930s, his father Jack being one of the two passed firemen who drove the branch train. He recollects Saturday mornings when blocks of ice, wrapped in hessian sacking, arrived in the guard's van and had to be delivered to the Merrythought Cafe on the High Street. John and his pal delivered the ice using a two wheeled railway owned 'spanker', taking turns to push it the three hundred yards or so to the cafe. The reward was a dish of ice cream smothered in raspberry sauce!

Living in Railway Cottages the railway was obviously a playground. Every night the engine fire was dropped and the pile of discarded ashes smouldered for days, providing the children with endless enjoyment by baking potatoes and apples in them. The railway could be a dangerous playground and so it proved for John's brother, who one day fell between the train and the platform as the train was leaving. No one saw him fall, but he had the presence of mind to get under the platform overhang until the train left. He emerged completely unscathed!

Jock Innes was a surfaceman who lived in a railway house at Avoch. Every day except Sunday he walked from Avoch to Muir of Ord carrying his hammer over his shoulder and a bag of spare wooden keys, tapping in loose keys as he went. He then took the train to Fortrose and finished his day by walking back to Avoch. Thus the whole branch was checked every day. He had an

unusual walking style, possibly caused by walking on the sleepers. His step length was governed by the space between the sleepers, which is not long enough for a normal step. Every time he brought his right foot forward his heels knocked together. This made a very distinctive easily identified sound when he walked and his boots wore out in an unusual place!

John had the occasional chance for a footplate trip, normally just shunting round the yard, but one evening the opportunity came to go with a special train of potatoes down to 'The Muir'. The engine was no 14392 *Loch Naver*. It was a pretty heavy train

The ticket window, in full working order, still remains inside Redcastle station building, now used by Nansen Highland. The polar bear recalls Fridtjof Nansen, one of the greatest Arctic explorers.   (*Jack Kernahan*)

to get up the hill out of Fortrose and a great thrill to be on an engine working hard. The abiding memory was of a hare which managed to get between the rails in front of the engine and had to run for miles before it finally managed to escape. The return was with empty vans for the next special.

On a summer afternoon in 1940, the Mackenzie family at no 2 and the MacBain family at no 3 were in front of their respective houses chatting over the garden fence. A German plane flew over from the direction of the Cromarty Firth and on towards Dalcross Aerodrome which was being built at that time. The plane was low enough for them to see the helmeted pilot in the cockpit when it passed between the water tower and the engine shed. Later it was established that it was a reconnaissance plane and was taking pictures of the flying boats moored off Fortrose. It was also reported that the plane was shot down.

That same afternoon Newfoundlanders were loading pit props into wagons in the goods yard. These men had been cutting trees in the woods at Blackstand. A rifle was discharged in the goods yard and the bullet broke the living room window at no 2. The families were still in their gardens when this happened and thankfully no one was hit.

In September 1940, John's father moved to Inverness as a driver. A railway van was dropped off on the turntable road, just outside the front gate of no 2 Railway Terrace, before the morning train left. With the help of railway staff the van was loaded with all the family's worldly goods. Wen the train returned it was shunted across the turntable while the engine was being turned and then coupled to the rear of the next train, in which the family, with the exception of Jack who was already at work in Inverness, travelled away from Fortrose. The van was attached to the rear of a train at Muir of Ord which reversed into platform 1 at Inverness for unloading on to a Wordie's horse drawn lorry for the final part of the journey to their new home.

Finally, Margaret Tanner, who as Margaret Smith was clerkess at Fortrose during the years 1941 to 1945, still vividly remembers the day when the following incident took place. The date is 'sometime during these years' and names have been omitted! Location names have been changed, but may just be easily recognised.

Once upon a time there was a wee branch line where an unco thing took place that's maybe worth the telling.

The last train from the main line station at Balbeastie was due back at the end of the line in Flowercastle at four in the afternoon. The station staff were anxious to get home for their tea once they had redded up the coaches and waiting room at the end of the day. And folk from the village were waiting anxiously for friends who had gone off to spend their silver in Affadear, the big town at the mouth of the Firth. They all waited and waited until a good forty five minutes behind time they heard a distant whistling and an anxious hooting. A minute later to a great blowing of smoke and hissing of steam the laggard train came into view.

The waiting folk stepped forward in anticipation. The station staff took hands from pooches and straightened their shoulders. Nearer and nearer came the great iron beast but to the amazement of all, with a wonderful squealing of brakes and spraying of sparks from locked wheels, the whole shebang shot past the platform and with a mighty bang hit the buffers designed to keep wandering trains out of the station master's tatties, snapdragons and geraniums.

Two sheepish heads leaned out of the cab above the footplate. With a now sensible slowness the train reversed back into the platform. Off came the passengers, looking gey shaken and glazed about the eyes. Last, off came the guard, hirpling on one good leg and sparing the other that had a thick white bandage round the ankle.

A view of Fortrose from the air showing the station at the top of the photograph which must have been taken before 1943 as the original engine shed can be seen. *(Groam House Museum)*

In the meantime the driver and fireman had uncoupled the engine, though they too looked a bit unsteady on their pins. They were hardly back in their cab and taking the loop line that would bring them to the turntable when, roused by the commotion, the driver's wife came out of her railway cottage. With arms folded over her pinny she marched towards the engine cab to see what was what. Now he was a wee futret of a fellow, the wife a hefty kind of quine, so, with a nervous look, he jumped down from the footplate to face the music.

I'll just need to get her turned ready for the morning," he began. But herself, sniffing on him something that was definitely not grease or engine oil, grabbed the back of his jacket and twisting the collar into a holding kind of knot, headed homewards with the words ringing out for all to hear : "You'll dee no such thing....not in the state you're in..." and with that the two of them disappeared into the house with a mighty slam of the front door. On the platform knowing grins were exchanged and ribs were nudged as the passengers, some of them with a good glow on their faces, started to tell their tale.

It seems that the station master down the line at Shooglie Brae had invited all aboard to step down and join him in a toast for his daughter's forthcoming wedding. The hospitality was taken and the drams were downed. Of course the crew were not to be left out. The only thing to fall by the wayside was the timetable. Well – almost the only thing. For when time was finally called and all were clambering back on board, the guard somehow missed his step as he swung up into his van, fell back and twisted his ankle. He was gathered up by a sympathetic crowd and stowed safely on board. There was no doctor to hand so another stop had to be made at Munlichty. Here a station trolley with three waggily wheels was commandeered to take him downhill to the surgery for treatment.

And some say that none of them touched another drop from that day on.

W A C Smith's Visit in 1959

W A C Smith photographed the branch goods train, worked by former Caledonian Railway '812' class 0-6-0 no 57594, on 25th August 1959.

Only four wagons on the outward journey at Redcastle.   *(W A C Smith/The Transport Treasury)*

At Munlochy on the outward journey.   *(W A C Smith/The Transport Treasury)*

The fireman has opened the gates at Corrachie crossing, between Munlochy and Avoch, to allow the short train to pass on its outward journey to Fortrose.   (W A C Smith /The Transport Treasury)

Shunting at Allangrange on the return journey, where the weeds were taking over. The building on the right, similar to ones at Munlochy and Avoch, housed the lever frames for operating the points and the ground signal.   (W A C Smith/The Transport Treasury)

57594 is oiled and watered after being turned at Fortrose.   *(W A C Smith/The Transport Treasury)*

Ready to depart back to Muir of Ord. The camping coach is sitting on the otherwise unused extension from the turntable road. 1959 was the final summer for this popular provision for visitors, first provided by the LMS and restored by British Railways in 1954.   *(W A C Smith/The Transport Treasury)*

CHAPTER 8

CLOSURE

As early as 1929, only 35 years after the branch opened, there was a threat of withdrawal of passenger services. In September of that year a deputation of officials from the LMS headquarters, accompanied by a local inspector, visited the line and carefully reviewed its income and expenditure, coming to the inevitable conclusion that it was too costly to continue operating the passenger service. Competing bus services were making inroads into the passenger traffic on branches to both Fortrose and Strathpeffer which was also under threat of closure. Road transport was still not available to handle heavy goods traffic, but passengers could be carried by bus, which would reduce the staff required to only a few needed to keep the permanent way to a sufficient standard to handle goods traffic. The uncertainty continued for a few months, with questions being asked in the House of Commons, the result of which was a statement to the effect that the Government was not prepared to award grants to continue services which were no longer economical. However the LMS relented and passenger services remained on both lines.

On 1st January 1948 the LMS Railway ceased to exist, after a relatively short existence of 25 years, and the Black Isle Railway became part of the nationalised British Railways. Unlike 1923 when the LMS undertook some improvements to the poor service which had been operated during the First World War, British Railways made no improvements. There continued to be only two trains daily, at 8.45 am on Mondays, Tuesdays and Wednesdays (9.5 am on the following three days) and 4.25 pm from Fortrose, returning at 3.35 pm and 5.40 pm from Muir of Ord. Saturday afternoon trips to Inverness were still possible with a 12.45 pm from Fortrose, returning at 9.15 pm. The run from Fortrose to Muir of Ord to form the 9.15 took passengers, leaving at 8.5 pm and calling only at Allangrange. The goods service left Muir of Ord at 11.30 am each morning Mondays to Saturdays, returning at 1.30 pm from Fortrose on Mondays to Fridays only, as on Saturdays the path was used by the 12.45 pm passenger train. The goods train on Saturday would have included the passenger coaches being returned to Fortrose to form the 12.45. There was also a goods train included in the timetable leaving Fortrose at 6 am, returning at 7 am, but this ran only if there was traffic requiring to be moved which could not wait until later in the day. Passengers arriving in Inverness by overnight trains, or indeed at any time in the morning, had to wait until 3 pm for a train with a connection at Muir of Ord for Fortrose. Anyone coming north by trains leaving Glasgow or Edinburgh in the afternoon had an overnight stay in Inverness except on a Saturday.

British Railways' District Traffic Superintendent at Inverness sought the views of Fortrose Town Council on the service for 1950. A request was made for a train from Muir of Ord connecting with the 10.40 am from Inverness, a train from Fortrose to connect with the 3.40 pm to the south from Muir of Ord and a train from Muir of Ord connecting from trains arriving in Inverness from the south in the evening. The response was that owing to the small number of passengers using the branch it would not be possible to introduce the improved service requested. The Council's views were forwarded to the BR offices and to the Tourist Board. The BR Chief Regional Officer in Glasgow reiterated the view that passenger numbers did not warrant additional services, and that alternative road services were available via both Muir of Ord and the Kessock Ferry. The Council responded by asking that he or his representative come to Fortrose to meet them and suggested that he try coming via the Kessock Ferry!

On 10th April the meeting took place, although it is not known how Mr Yeaman, District Superintendent, and Mr McDiarmid from Inverness travelled to Fortrose. The first train from Muir of Ord, of course, was not until 3.35 pm, so they would appreciate the impracticalities of rail travel to Black Isle stations. The Council emphasised the inconveniences and inadequacy of the service, while Mr Yeaman again indicated the lack of public patronage. He finally stated that he would suggest that a connection be provided from Muir of Ord in the forenoon, but at the cost of discontinuing the afternoon train (the 3.35 pm) and the consequent running of the goods train in the afternoon instead of the morning. The Council agreed to write to the Highland Transport Company requesting a through bus from Inverness to Fortrose shortly after the arrival of trains from Aberdeen at 6.5 pm and the south at 8.1 pm. Buses were introduced from Muir of Ord to Fortrose in the evening providing a connection with afternoon trains arriving from the south.

Alterations to the service were made from 5th June. The 3.15 pm from Muir of Ord and the 4.25 pm (Saturdays excepted) from Fortrose were replaced by an 11.15 am from Muir of Ord which connected out of the 10.40 am Inverness to Wick, and the 12.45 pm from Fortrose ran daily rather than only on Saturdays. It connected into the 12.5 pm from Tain, giving an arrival into Inverness at 2.1 pm. The 12.45 pm was therefore the last train of the day from Fortrose, and it was still impossible for a daily visitor to have more than an hour in the town. Unfortunately the decision to make these changes was made too late for them to be included

'Small Ben' no 14397 Ben y'Gloe *ready to depart from Fortrose for Muir of Ord in the late 1940s. One corridor coach is sufficient for the low numbers of passengers now expected.*

(Highland Railway Society)

	Muir of Ord and Fortrose—WEEKDAYS ONLY Table 121						B	A	Sats only		Sats only
Mls		p.m	p.m	Sats only p.m			a.m	a.m	p.m	p.m	p.m
..	Muir of Ord ..lev.	3 15	5 40	9 25	Fortrose .... lev.		8 45	9 5	1245	1 25	3 15
3¾	Redcastle	3 23	5 50	9 35	Avoch		8 53	) 11	1251	1 31	..
5¾	Allangrange	3 28	5 58	9 41	Munlochy		9 3	) 18	1258	4 3(	..
8	Munlochy	3 33	6 10	9 47	Allangrange		9 15	) 2(	1 4	4 4(	8 46
11¼	Avoch	3 39	6 26	9 54	Redcastle		9 25	) 31	1 11	4 51	..
13½	Fortrose .. arr.	3 45	6 37	10 0	Muir of Ord ..arr.		9 35	) 4(	1 2(	5 0	9 5

Public timetable for Summer 1950

in the printed summer timetable and they appeared only in the amendments leaflets, with the result that they were virtually unknown south of Inverness. These changes, of course, had been done with no extra train mileage and at no additional cost. There was one further additional service operated, however, as a connection was provided on Saturdays at 11 pm from Muir of Ord, connecting out of the 10.30 pm Inverness to Tain, thus giving passengers from the Black Isle a real opportunity for a Saturday evening in Inverness. This extra train would have entailed additional costs, not only in the mileage costs for a double run of the branch train, but in an extra hour and a half overtime payments for station and engine staff. This may well have been only a locally authorised venture, as it did not appear in the official timetable amendment sheet, nor did it appear to be advertised locally. On 11th September the District Traffic Inspector at Inverness wrote to the Council stating that the new Saturdays only train at 11 pm from Muir of Ord to Fortrose had been taken off owing to lack of patronage. The Council continued to be critical of British Railways regarding the failure of the railway authorities to give the public adequate information regarding the new services put on during the summer

From 25th September 1950 the timetable changed with trains now leaving Fortrose at 8.50 am Monday to Wednesday and 9.10 am Thursday to Saturday, and 1 pm (1.20 pm on Saturdays). Muir of Ord departures were 11.15 am and 5.40 pm. On Saturdays there were additional services from Fortrose at 4.25 pm and 8.15 pm, the latter calling only at Allangrange, and returning with those enjoying their afternoon and early evening in Inverness at 9.20 pm from Muir of Ord. This service continued until the withdrawal of passenger services. Handbills were produced advertising a special excursion to Inverness from Fortrose and Avoch, at a return fare of 2/6 on Tuesdays and Thursdays on the 1 pm from Fortrose, returning from Inverness at 5 pm, and on Saturdays by the 1.20 pm, returning at either 5 pm or 8.45 pm, change at Muir of Ord being necessary on all services.

It was not long before the inevitable happened. At the beginning of March 1951 British Railways intimated their intention to withdraw passenger services from the branch. Passenger receipts in the last year had amounted to only £2,576, less than £50 per week, while parcels receipts were slightly higher at £2,978. After taking into account savings in staff costs, train working and track and other maintenance costs a saving of around £7,000 per annum was anticipated. Fortrose Town Council were vociferous in their opposition but there does not appear to have been much local opposition. The County Council decided not to object in view of the small numbers using the trains. Public support of the service was described as 'inadequate'. The poor level of the service and the state of the trains did nothing to encourage passengers.

There was little to attract passengers. It was effectively impossible for anyone wishing to visit anywhere on the branch on a day trip to have any time in Black Isle villages, and the carriages were not conducive to a pleasant journey. One intrepid traveller, 'Frozen Out' of Fortrose, attempted the trip in May 1951, and expressed his comments in a letter to the editor of the Ross-shire Journal:

As a passenger at Muir of Ord, we were shown two lonely carriages without an engine or heating of any kind. As we entered the carriage we were disgusted at the condition of it. To sit down we had to put our macintoshes on the seat owing to the dust. In this appalling state we had to wait twenty minutes before the engine linked on. Make the trains clean warm and comfortable and you will get the support of the public.

At a meeting of the British Transport Commission held on 29th May 1951 approval in principle was given to the Railway Executive's recommendations for withdrawal of a large number of unremunerative branch line services, including the Fortrose branch. The chairman raised the question:

Before action is actually taken on some of the more important cases in this list (which included eleven in Scotland, one of which was Fortrose) will it not be expedient to refer to the Consultative Committee of Users?

A manuscript note on the minute is interesting :

Scottish Area CC has always supported the British Transport Commission and the Railway Executive 100% on withdrawal of passenger services on unprofitable branch lines provided alternative road services are available. The Chairman of the Committee has been in close touch with Cameron and Amos. I see no reason therefore to hold up action by the Railway Executive but if you wish them to notify to Scottish CC as a matter of courtesy there would be no objection.

Thomas Cameron was the Railway Executive's Chief Regional Officer for Scotland and James Amos was chairman of the Scottish Omnibuses Group. It would appear that the Railway Executive had little cause for concern that the Consultative Committee would force them to continue the passenger service.

The Town Council's objections were put in a letter to the Scottish Transport Users' Consultative Committee who had to decide whether hardship would be caused by the withdrawal of the passenger service. In their letter of objection the council indicated that no real effort had been made to provide a satisfactory rail service at a reasonable cost, nor had there been any form of cooperation between the Railway Executive and the bus company. Buses left Fortrose for Inverness at the same time as two of the trains, while at Muir of Ord buses competed with the rail service at the same hours. Neither bus nor train service

The last passenger train to leave Fortrose on Saturday 29th September 1951. Back row : Malcolm Macleod, Frankie Hay (who had been a driver on the branch since Highland Railway days), Jimmy Leitch. Front row : C MacBain, Jock Gordon, Molly Gordon (Jock's wife and a former goods clerkess), Ephie Sinclair, J Fraser, J Sutherland (station master) and A Urquhart. A sad day for them all, as thereafter the railway community at Fortrose ceased to exist.
(Avoch Heritage Association)

One of the two Caledonian Railway rebuilt Dunalastair IV 4-4-0s, no 54439, outside the replacement engine shed at Fortrose on 30th July 1949
(Neville Stead collection)

provided reasonable connections for passengers desiring to travel from the Black Isle to the south by any train of the day from Inverness. Fortrose was a holiday resort, much frequented by visitors from the south. Major problems were anticipated for passengers having to carry luggage, which the buses were ill fitted to transport, between trains and buses at Inverness, and again where a change of buses was required at Muir of Ord involving a walk of a hundred yards. The Council quoted the words of the speech introducing the Transport Bill in 1946:

Travel in this country is becoming a disagreeable thing, something to be endured. The commissioners have to see that all parts of the country are adequately served. Rural areas have never had the transport facilities they need. There are no physical or financial reasons why we should not have the most efficient, comfortable, speedy and cheap system of transport in the world.

These points were put by the Consultative Committee to the Highland Transport Company which operated the bus service. The response was that there were reasonable connections out of the Fortrose buses for passengers wishing to travel south from Inverness and that having regard to the relatively small number of passengers travelling to and from the Black Isle compared with main road traffic passing through Muir of Ord they did not admit that a through service between Fortrose and Inverness was necessary. As far as luggage was concerned no complaints had ever been received concerning lack of luggage accommodation on any of the company's existing routes. It was not possible for buses to be brought into Station Square at Inverness, but agreement had recently been reached for the provision of a central station at Farraline Park for all bus operators. This was not a great distance from the railway station. They also pointed out that, following representations made by the Fortrose Town Clerk, they had agreed, during the summer of 1950, to hold until 9.20 pm their 8.50 pm bus from Muir of Ord for connecting passengers from the 8.45 pm train from Inverness. During this period not more than an average of 5.1 persons per week made use of the connection. In other words, for the convenience of less than one person per night from the train not less than 24 bus passengers, and often well over 30, were kept waiting half an hour, a delay which gave rise to much inconvenience. It had therefore been decided that during the 1951 summer the connection would be made only on Thursdays (the Fortrose half-holiday) and Saturdays.

Fortrose Town Council responded by stating that no one burdened by luggage, particularly with the conditions prevailing at Inverness and Muir of Ord where there was no shelter, would take the bus if they could help it. They accepted that the travelling public, at least the short distance traveller, had forsaken the train for the bus, but that this was due largely to the raising of rail fares and the failure to provide a convenient service. They pointed out that the name 'Fortrose' had already been removed from the destination board at Inverness station, and suggested that buses could enter Station Square if the South African War Memorial was moved.

The Consultative Committee considered that the responses from the bus company adequately addressed the concerns of the Town Council and pointed out that if people did not use the trains the passenger service must of necessity be withdrawn. Complaints regarding the closure of branch lines were being made regardless of the question of economics. The committee stated that they had considered very carefully the representations made to them by the Town Council but agreed unanimously that they considered that the proposed alternative services were reasonable and that they would not oppose the withdrawal of the passenger train service. Formal withdrawal took place with effect from Monday 1st October 1951, the last trains running the previous Saturday, 29th September.

By this time most of the former Highland Railway engines associated with the branch throughout its life had been withdrawn. The last of the 'Yankee' tanks, the former *Munlochy* as LMS no 15014, ran 754,221 miles between 1906 when it was reboilered and its withdrawal in 1934, an average of over 500 miles per week, much of its work being on the Black Isle line. The last of the 'Skye Bogies', by then numbered 14277, and nicknamed *Queen Mary*, possibly saw

Former Caledonian Railway '652' class 0-6-0, a modernised version of the '812' class, built in 1909, originally Caledonian Railway no 326 and now British Railways 57642 was an Inverness engine for much of the 1950s until reallocated to Stirling in March 1959. During the previous summer it is seen at the throat of Fortrose goods yard. Note the brake van left on the single line. When the return train is made up and placed in an adjacent siding the handbrake will be released and the brake van will roll by gravity to the end of the platform road before the train is shunted onto it for the return journey to Inverness.
(SRPS/Roy M Crombie)

All engines on the branch used the turntable at Fortrose. 57642 is turned before it takes its train back to Inverness in the summer of 1958. Note the camping coach in the track beyond the turntable.
(SRPS/Roy M Crombie)

out its final days on the line until its withdrawal at the end of 1929. The 'Lochs' had gone by 1950, and only four 'Small Bens' made it into the 1950s, but several were recorded on the Black Isle line after the war. However, by the time the line closed to passenger traffic the service was run by former Caledonian Railway 3P 4-4-0s, nine of which were allocated to Inverness in 1950. One of these hauled the last timetabled passenger train.

The replacement bus service consisted of six services to and from Inverness via Muir of Ord, plus a late night bus on Thursdays and Saturdays, and four each day via the Kessock Ferry. The remaining goods train service ran from Inverness, so there was no need for operating staff at Fortrose where the engine shed was closed. It is likely that Frankie Hay, by that time aged 64, retired, having spent over half his life on the branch since Highland Railway days. He died in 1976, aged 89. Jimmy Leitch, who had started on the railway at Inverness in 1938, had come to Fortrose in 1943 after a few years on the Inverness to Perth line. He had been passed as a driver at the early age of 22, two years before he came to Fortrose in 1943. After the passenger closure he returned to Inverness but left railway service in 1957. He died in 2003 at the age of 84.

The Town Council had put up a good fight, but were not yet finished. On 10th March 1952 letters were sent to the Minister of Transport and to the Secretary of State for Scotland. Their complaint was that representations had been made to various bodies but they 'might as well never have been made at all'. They considered that the Railway Executive had made up their minds to withdraw the service and were not to be budged from it. They had succeeded in impressing their view of the case upon all other parties concerned other than themselves. The Transport Users' Consultative Committee had given no adequate consideration to the matter. The very fact that they had entered into no discussion of the points at issue with the Council was demonstrated as sufficient proof of this. Their opinion of the TUCC was that the

Former Caledonian Railway '812' class 0-6-0 no 57594 ready to leave Fortrose with a single wagon goods train on 21st October 1959. The agent's house can be seen in the background. The platform has been substantially shortened and a concrete edge installed following the withdrawal of passenger services some eight years earlier.   (Roy Hamilton)

Committee was 'inadequate, impotent and futile'. No bus service, however much improved, could take the place of the rail service, particularly for tourists and summer visitors. The Secretary of State was asked if there was any assistance he could give in having the decision reconsidered and the passenger service restored, at least in the summer months.

Concern by the TUCC about the attitude of the Town Council, which had also been made public through a letter from the Town Clerk appearing in *The Scotsman* newspaper of 10th August 1951 to the tone of which the Commission Chairman had taken exception, resulted in an offer being made to the Council for a meeting. This was arranged for 6th May, but the illness of the Provost and the unavailability of one of the Council's representatives resulted in a request for postponement of the meeting. On 27th May the Town Clerk wrote stating that as certain alterations had been promised to the bus service between Inverness and Fortrose which would, to a large extent, meet the position created by the withdrawal of the passenger train service the Council would no longer require a meeting with the Committee. The service alterations and the introduction of new buses with adequate accommodation for luggage took place from 16th June 1952.

The railway had deserted the passengers by providing an inadequate and expensive service, so the passengers deserted the railway for the bus, so, in turn, the railway totally deserted the passengers by withdrawing the service.

The line continued in operation for goods traffic and for passengers' luggage in advance services, although no passengers could actually travel from branch stations. The post offices remained at Redcastle and Allangrange, officially named Killearnan and Tore respectively, while at Redcastle John Mackenzie, the last station master, continued looking after the railway sack hire business conducted from the station. Lorries for onward delivery and collection were based at Avoch and Fortrose. The goods handled continued to be similar to that handled in earlier years, principally agriculture based plus domestic coal. Hay, seed potatoes and grain from the big farms between Fortrose and Cromarty were major seasonal exports requiring special trains. In 1958 2,505 tons of coal came into Fortrose, 35 tons into Munlochy and 914 tons into Redcastle. A camping coach was again provided annually from 1954, situated on the extension of the turntable track. Campers used the toilet facilities in the station building. The usual condition attaching to the use of the coach, namely that a railway ticket to the station where the coach was sited be purchased, could not be implemented. Rail travel to Muir of Ord was all that could be expected.

One physical change was made to the stations after passenger closure. It was intended when the line was built that the platform edges would be made of four inch thick Caithness pavement coping stones. The platform edges at Munlochy, Avoch and Fortrose actually comprised only longitudinal wooden boards while the passenger service operated. During the 1950s the platforms were all shortened to extend for little more than the area adjacent to the buildings, and all were edged with concrete. The engine shed at Fortrose was no longer required as the goods traffic was worked from Muir of Ord, and was soon dismantled. Shortly after the withdrawal of the passenger service Mr MacGillivray, the last station master and post master at Allangrange, moved the post office to a small shop he had constructed at Heathpark. Despite being repainted in the summer of 1953 the building at Allangrange was no longer required after the station became an unstaffed public siding on 7th March 1955 and in 1957 it was dismantled and sold to a local purchaser. All the other station buildings remained until the complete closure of the line.

Throughout the life of the line attention had been paid through regular inspections to the bridges on the line, with routine pointing and replacement of coping stones where required.

Munlochy on 16th April 1957, with a barrow load of boxes awaiting the goods train. The goods shed had been removed in 1954. The platform edge was rebuilt in concrete after the passenger closure.

(James L Stevenson)

Redcastle on 16th April 1957. The platforms at all the stations were shortened after the passenger closure.   *(James L Stevenson)*

Allangrange on 16th April 1957. It is likely that the wagons are stored rather than indicating a large volume of traffic   *(James L Stevenson)*

Allangrange looking towards Munlochy on 16th April 1957. The station building was repainted in 1953, after the passenger closure, and was sold in 1957. *(James L Stevenson)*

The only girder bridge, at Linnie, was repainted in 1938. The bridge which required most attention was that over the Avoch Burn. The unusual low level brick arch had required repair in 1915 when a few of the bricks on the under side were found to be decaying and weep holes on the eastern side were causing more harm than good. Repairs to the arch stones and parapet walls took place in 1947 and 1948, but in 1953 the footpath bridge attached to the side of the bridge was in need of urgent repair, while the lattice girder forming the outside parapet and the whole of the steelwork supports were badly in need of cleaning and painting. In September 1959 authority was given for the removal of the footpath bridge, by then considered to be in a dangerous condition, together with the access stairway from Mackenzie Place, but they were still in place when the line was closed the following year. Fortrose goods shed was removed in the summer of 1959, the crane inside the building being taken for use at the harbour.

During the late 1950s proposals were put forward for rationalisation of railway services north of Inverness, involving the closure of many little used stations. A late addition to the proposals, in March 1959, was the complete closure of the Fortrose branch. The Town Council once more attempted to stop the closure, suggesting that what was required to put Fortrose and Rosemarkie properly on the map as increasingly popular resorts was a fast and efficient passenger and freight service from Inverness. They suggested that Fortrose station remain unstaffed and that fast diesel or electric cars with a conductor on board should run direct to Inverness. There was little chance of that happening and complete closure was approved on 17th July 1959. To overcome objections about the seasonal potato traffic, British Railways agreed to convey that traffic free of charge to Muir of Ord for five years after closure.

The last goods train left Fortrose during the afternoon of Saturday 11th June 1960. Flags had flown on the day the line opened. One solitary flag, at the King George VI playing field, was flown at half mast when the last train left. But it was not to be the very last. Although

The final train on the branch, the railtour on 14th June 1960 hauled by former Caledonian Railway '812' class 0-6-0 no 57594, crosses the Avoch Burn on its return journey to Muir of Ord. Note the cantilevered bridge carrying the footpath from the village to the station.   (Highland Railway Society)

The last goods train appears lengthy as it is clearing all remaining wagons from the branch on 11th June 1960. The boys witnessing a sad piece of local history being made at Munlochy are Peter Macleman, Andrew Jack Ross and Allan Ross.   (Avoch Heritage Association)

The crew of former Caledonian Railway '812' class no 57594 at Munlochy on Saturday 11th June 1960 on the last goods train on the branch. The driver (on the left) is E MacIntosh, while John Docherty, the last member of staff at Munlochy, hands a letter to the guard.

(Avoch Heritage Association)

the official closure was with effect from Monday 13th June, on the following day the line was visited in the late afternoon by a passenger train in the form of a five coach railtour. Just as the opening of the line had been celebrated a day late due to the Fast Day holiday on 1st February 1894, so the closure was also a day late. The last goods train and the railtour were hauled by former Caledonian Railway '812' class 3F 0-6-0 no 57594, built in 1900 and sent north to Inverness in October 1957. The turntable, ever a source of fascination for the children, continued in use until the last day.

Throughout the 1950s the goods trains, with speed on the branch limited to 30 mph, had been worked principally by the '812' 0-6-0s. Although new diesels in the form of BRCW Type 2s (later Class 26) and English Electric Type 1s (later Class 20) had arrived at Inverness in March 1960, it is highly unlikely that any diesel ever worked on the branch prior to closure. Indeed probably no BR standard engines were seen at Fortrose, and, with the exception of the Stanier 2-6-2 tank which appeared briefly in 1939, it is probable that the line saw nothing but pre-grouping engines.

The level crossing gates at Corrachie, between Munlochy and Avoch, are closed against the railway for the last time following the passage of the last train on 14th June 1960. The crossing keeper's cottage is still standing.

(R M Casserley)

The branch signal at Muir of Ord is pulled off for the last time to allow former Caledonian Railway '812'
class 0-6-0 no 57594 on to the Black Isle line with the last train on Tuesday 14th June 1960.
(HRS collection

In 1951 Fortrose Town Council had approached British Railways in an attempt to have the
closed station facilities made available as public conveniences, but the level of rental requested,
plus the condition that an attendant be provided, resulted in the idea not being pursued. An
alternative was the construction in 1953 at a cost of £571.17.1d of a new purpose built facility
in Station Road, still in use today.

Even before the last train ran, Fortrose Town Council were considering the station site for a
new fire station, and another party was interested in using the area as a lime dump. Following
complete closure the Council attempted to purchase the station buildings, the six cottages, the
agent's house and eleven acres of land. The District Valuer put a price of £2,500 on the assets
while BR's Estate and Rating Surveyor considered the value to be £4,151. Permitted uses of
the ground were residential, shopping, business and small industrial premises. The houses

The Fortrose turntable
was used right up to
the last day. Former
Caledonian Railway
'812' class no 57594
was the final engine
to use it, on 14th June
1960, a day after the
formal closure, on the
SLS/RCTS railtour
which closed the
branch.

(R M Casserley)

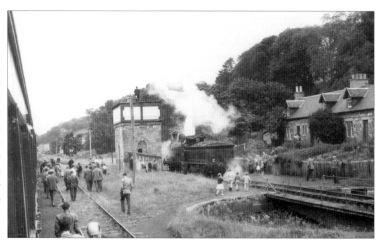

Delivered new to Inverness a few weeks earlier, English Electric Type 1 Bo-Bo no D8034 at the north end of Muir of Ord station in April 1960. The engine did not work the branch goods train that day, and it is unlikely that any diesel engine was ever on the Black Isle branch.

(Norris Forrest/The Transport Treasury)

appeared to be in good order although there were no bathrooms. Electric lighting had been installed some years before. At a meeting on 4th September Bailie McCombie thought that the waiting rooms would make suitable council offices, but Bailie Mackenzie considered that they were too far from the main street. It was agreed to open negotiations for purchase. The Treasurer moved against this but did not find a seconder. Word of the council's interest got round the town and within a week an unlikely source of funding for the project arose. Miss Isa Ross, who kept a shop in the town centre, offered to pay for the land and buildings by means of a gift of £4,150 on certain conditions. Firstly the station master's house was to be sold on to a friend of hers for £2,000. The existing station building was to be used as council offices. The area of the station was to be used for car parking and the existing official car park in Cathedral Square, opposite her house, was to be closed. Finally, Miss Ross being a staunch supporter of the Church of Scotland, no gambling establishment was to be permitted in the area and no desecration of the Sabbath would be allowed. Unfortunately in December British Railways, despite two official valuations well below the figure, asked an increased price of £6,500, at which the Town Clerk informed them that the council was no longer interested and Miss Ross turned her munificence in another direction.

In time a fire station was built on the site of the station building, the land levelled and car parking provided on the land east of the new fire station. The houses all remain, 1 to 6 Railway Terrace now being renumbered in the opposite direction as 10 to 5 Station Crescent.

Being rich farming country much of the trackbed has been reclaimed and has disappeared into adjacent fields, but just over five miles are easily walkable, particularly between Muir of Ord and Redcastle through Spital Wood, and through Craig Wood between Avoch and

Fortrose. The largest survivor is the station building at Redcastle, beautifully painted in LMS colours, and now used by Nansen Highland. This organisation, originally motivated by the life of the Norwegian humanitarian and explorer Fridtjof Nansen, provides training for young adults with learning and related difficulties. The other station building which survives, although scarcely recognisable, is Avoch, totally rebuilt into a house in the late 1960s. The former crossing keepers' cottages at Linnie near Redcastle, and Corrachie between Munlochy and Avoch are still extant. The embankment at the back of Munlochy village is still pierced by the culvert for the burn, but the arch shown under construction in 1892 in the photograph on page 34 is no longer visible, being covered by a curtain of ivy. At the other side, however, can be seen the stonework, and, high on the east side, the date 1946 engraved in the concrete, confirming the date when the wing walls and the parapet were renewed. At Avoch the bridge over the burn with the reinforcing brick arch remains, but the bridge itself, with one of the parapets non-existent, is highly dangerous and securely bricked off. The site of Allangrange station is in use for light industry and bus parking, while housing occupies the sites of the stations and goods yards at Munlochy, Avoch, and Fortrose, but each has a Station Road and in addition Munlochy has a Station Brae and Court, Avoch still has the Station Hotel and Fortrose the Station Square and Crescent. The only relic at Fortrose, other than the houses, is the 20 ton weighbridge, the brick construction betraying its installation during the Second World War when it replaced an earlier 7½ ton one. The station masters' houses all remain, while 'The Cabin', incorporating the signal cabin originally at Fortrose station, still stands in Rosemarkie.

The final mention of the branch on British Railways was not until 1970, ten years after the line closed, when boxes of fish were regularly sent, according to the consignment notes, to Avoch station for Gilbert Skinner the fishmonger. They would, of course, be taken by road from Muir of Ord. Ironically, one of the benefits supposed to flow from the railway was to be to take fish from Avoch, but the distance of the station from the harbour and the fact that most Avoch fishermen landed their catches at Inverness meant that this did not happen.

The trains may be long gone, but the Black Isle Railway is still fondly remembered by many of the senior citizens, and is a source of interest and enquiry by some of the younger.

Avoch station building was converted to a dwelling house in the late 1960s and remains so today.

(Author's collection)

The exterior of Fortrose station on 25th August 1959. The British Railways local delivery lorry carried traffic which was brought on the branch freight train. (W A C Smith/The Transport Treasury)

The crossing keeper's cottage at Linnie, east of Redcastle, is still in existence. (Jack Kernahan)

APPENDIX 1 : BRIDGES

All bridges are constructed of stone and brick, except No.13 which is of steel girders.

No.	Over/ under railway	Grid ref (NH)	Span (feet)	Dist from Muir of Ord	Description	Current State
1	Over	532505	15	0½	Occupation road	Demolished
2	Under	545505	20	1¼	Public road to Culbokie	Demolished
3	Under	546505	10	1½	Occupation road	Extant
4	Under	548505	12		Occupation road	Extant
5	Over	554503	15	1¾	Occupation road	Extant
6	Under	562503	10	2¼	Creep at Spittal Wood	Extant
7	Under	565504	10	2½	Creep at Spittal Wood	Extant
8	Under	569506	12	2¾	Occupation road	Extant
9	Under	572506	7	3	Creep	Extant
10	Over	576508	15	3¼	Occupation road	Extant
11	Over	582511	15	3¾	Public road at Redcastle station	Filled in
12	Under	592514	4	4¼	Culvert at Linnie	Extant
13	Under	593515	40	4½	Public road at Linnie (steel)	Demolished
14	Under	597517	12	4¾	Access road to Linnie Farm	Extant
15	Under	598518	4		Culvert at Linnie Farm	Demolished
16	Over	610519	18.5	5½	Public road at Allangrage station	Filled in
17	Over	624524	15	6½	Occupation road	Extant
18	Over	635528	15	7¼	Public road at Drummore	Extant
19	Under	639530	4	7½	Over Little Burn	Extant
20	Under	644532	16	7¾	Public road to Littleburn	Filled in
21	Under	645533	15		Over Munlochy Burn	Extant
22	Over	646534	26	8	Public road at Munlochy station	Filled in
23	Over	650536	15	8¼	Public road at Viewmount	Filled in
24	Under	655537	12	8½	Occupation road	Demolished
25	Under	657538	12	8¾	Occupation road	Demolished
26	Under	661539	12		Occupation road	Extant
27	Over	663539	15	9	Public road at Gateside Farm	Filled in
28	Over	691554	15	11	Public Fortrose road at Avoch	Filled in (parapets extant)
29	Under	696554	20	11¼	Over Avoch Burn	Extant
30	Over	699553	21	11½	Mackenzie Place at Avoch	Demolished
31	Under	701552	12	12	Public road at Geddeston	Extant
32	Under	713557	4	12½	Over Redgowan Burn	Extant
33	Under	717560	8	12¾	Culvert	Extant
34	Under	720562	6	13	Over Craig Burn	Extant
35	Under	724565	20	13¼	Over Bishops Road, Fortrose	Extant

The demolition of the bridge taking Mackenzie Place over the line east of the burn at Avoch. It was originally intended that this be a girder bridge. There was a flight of steps to a footpath along the south side of the line and over the burn to give a short cut for passengers to the station. Only four overbridges, in remote areas, remain, the others having been infilled. (*Avoch Heritage Association*)

APPENDIX 2 : STATIONS AND SIDINGS

	From Muir of Ord		Grid ref	Station ticket code numbers	
	Miles	Yards	(NH)	HR	LMSR
Muir of Ord			527501	49	4649
Spital Wood Siding	1	780	555504		
Redcastle	3	1110	582511	50	4650
Allangrange	5	672	609519	51	4651
Redburn Wood Siding	6	1147	628526		
Munlochy	7	1622	647534	52	4652
Rosehaugh Halt	10	754	682549		
Avoch	11	354	695553	53	4653
Fortrose	13	780	725567	54	4654

BIBLIOGRAPHY

Cromarty & Dingwall Light Railway, Eric H Malcolm, Cromarty Courthouse, 1993, ISBN 1 89841602 8.

Highland Railway, David Ross, Stenlake Publishing, 2010, ISBN 9781840334975.

Highland Railway Albums, Volumes 1 and 2, Anthony J Lambert, Ian Allan, 1974, ISBN 071100532X and 1978, ISBN 0711008779, respectively.

Highland Railway, Its Constituents and Successors, Stephenson Locomotive Society, 1955.

Highland Railway Locomotives, Books 1 and 2, Cormack and Stevenson, RCTS, 1988, ISBN 0 90115 64 9 and ISBN 0 901115 72 X.

Highland Railway : People and Places, Neil T Sinclair, Breedon Books, 2005, ISBN 1 85983 453 1.

Highland Railway Journal, Highland Railway Society, various issues.

History of the Highland Railway, by H.A. Vallance, updated by Clinker and Lambert as *The Highland Railway*, House of Lochar, ISBN 1 899863 07 9.

LMS Engine Sheds, Volume 6, Hawkins, Reeve and Stevenson, Irwell Press 1989, ISBN 1 871608 04X.

Lost Stations on the Far North Line, Keith Fenwick, Neil T Sinclair and Richard Ardern, Highland Railway Society, 2010, ISBN 978095454854 4.

Regional History of the Railways of Great Britain, Volume 15, North of Scotland, John Thomas and David Turnock, David St John Thomas, ISBN 0946537 03 8.

THE HIGHLAND RAILWAY SOCIETY

The Highland Railway Society caters for all those interested in the varied aspects of the railway, including its predecessors and its successors to the present day.

An illustrated quarterly *Journal* is distributed to members and contains a wide variety of articles and information. Members queries are a regular feature and details of new books, videos and models of interest are reported. An active Internet chat group stimulates discussion among members. The Society's publications include a series of books commemorating the 150th anniversaries of the opening of various sections of the system.

Meetings are held in both Scotland and England. An Annual Gathering is held each September and includes a full day of talks, films, etc., as well as an opportunity to meet fellow members.

The Society has Library, Photographic and Drawing collections which are available to members. Copies of drawings are available for purchase. Modellers are well catered for. Complete kits are produced in limited runs. Specially commissioned modelling components such as axle boxes, buffers and springs are available, plus a comprehensive set of transfers to enable any Highland loco to be named.

Membership details can be found on the our website at www.hrsoc.org.uk.